Sexual Forensics

Sexual Forensics

Lust, Passion, and Psychopathic Killers

Don Jacobs and Ashleigh Portales

 PRAEGER

AN IMPRINT OF ABC-CLIO, LLC
Santa Barbara, California • Denver, Colorado • Oxford, England

Library of Congress Cataloging-in-Publication Data

Jacobs, Donald Trent, 1946-
    Sexual forensics : lust, passion, and psychopathic killers / Don Jacobs and Ashleigh Portales.
        pages cm
    Includes bibliographical references and index.
    ISBN 978-1-4408-0430-4 (alk. paper) — ISBN 978-1-4408-0431-1 (ebook)
    1. Crimes of passion. I. Portales, Ashleigh. II. Title.
    HV6053.J33 2014
        363.25'953—dc23   2014000007

ISBN: 978-1-4408-0430-4
EISBN: 978-1-4408-0431-1

18 17 16 15 14   1 2 3 4 5

This book is also available on the World Wide Web as an eBook.
Visit www.abc-clio.com for details.

Praeger
An Imprint of ABC-CLIO, LLC

ABC-CLIO, LLC
130 Cremona Drive, P.O. Box 1911
Santa Barbara, California 93116-1911

This book is printed on acid-free paper ∞

Manufactured in the United States of America

Contents

A smooth-talking, handsome, and charming male can effectively disguise harming behaviors of pathology, perversion, and violence, thus in the end, blindsiding targeted prey. . . . In navigating life's relationship intricacies we learn performances can be nothing more than "auditions" from ancient survival scripts. So, in modern neuropsychology, we must be prepared to address behavior as a clue. By reading even a few pages in a book we can gain valuable insights saving ourselves and loved ones the experience of a living nightmare.

Don Jacobs 2013

Preface

HOW CAN SO MUCH HARM COME FROM SO MUCH CHARM?

Sexual forensics is the analysis of sexual crimes from crime-scene evidence applied to known-offender characteristics (KOC) in order to understand the etiology of criminal minds. In short, it tells us how two mutually enjoyable states—lust and passion—became corrupted in the criminal mind to include horrific violence and murder. When lust and passion begin to turn violent, normal sexual foreplay becomes perverted in criminal minds, particularly psychopathic minds, leading to variations of such pre-crime stalking offenses as voyeurism with masturbation. As the corruption mounts, the carry-through is characterized by rape, torture and mutilation, and, ultimately, disposal of the victim's body.

This volume introduces readers to what I call *neurotruth* (Jacobs 2011), the neuropsychological truths about our species that rarely if ever vary. Such truths have largely been discovered through technological research using high-definition brain scans and other controlled studies, some of which are documented in the chapters that follow.

Neurotruth speaks volumes about neuroscience, which documents that lust stems from biological variations (or "pedigrees") in neurotransmitters in the brain and neurohormones in the body. Both lust and passion are what I call vigorous brain conditions, affecting modern behavior evolved from ancient survival scripts. From such scripts come lustful flirting, "posturing," and selection of a mate, leading ultimately to the creation of progeny and the continuation of our species.

When corruption, perversion, and arrogance dominate in the brain, as we will show, warning signs (or "red flags") of impending harmful actions must be interpreted. Thus investigative sciences, especially forensic neuropsychology, are among the most important applied sciences of the 21st century. Red flags are visible signs of invisible motivations from potential predators who "audition" before prey. Are they just exhibiting harmless flirtatious behavior or does their behavior foretell the darker designs of a "Jekyll and Hyde" nature to be unveiled later in perverted and violent actions? What methods and behavior do they use to blindside their victims?

Potential prey lucky enough to avoid meeting such predators may be tempted to ask how so much harm could come from so much charm. The answer is one of our strongest messages, requiring 21st-century knowledge of the Jekyll and Hyde types that appear so charming in initial interactions. Modern lessons taken from profiles in each chapter document the central importance of paying attention to red flags from those who seek to engage us in sexual scenarios. The primary purpose of this book is to help readers understand the difference between normal passion and lust directed toward positive ends and corruptive, perverted, and pathological passion and lust.

Here's a question I ask on the very first day of my forensic psychology classes at Weatherford College: "Did you ever play with neighborhood kids who you knew, even when you were a young child, would eventually spend time in prison?" Instantly, some students nod affirmatively. So even children can acknowledge the meaning of red flags. Without knowing how or why, both children and adults just know something is wrong, something is not quite right. The vital alarm system that alerts us to red flags is discussed in chapter 4.

The essence of neurotruth is found in behavioral displays tied to vigorous brain conditions defining our species' tendencies to act in highly predictable ways (Jacobs 2011). Just as dark clouds and strong winds warn us of approaching storms, so must we come to recognize red flags warning us of maladapted behavior in individuals who stand before us—in spite of the prosocial behavior that often hides the "trapdoor spider" beneath the charm.

Acknowledgments

Thanks to my top students for your brilliant ideas and suggestions in the preparation of our text. Also, special thanks to tech wizard John Wyatt for saving our manuscript from deletion a couple of times and for his expertise in the final presentation of our text.

PART I

Sexual Forensics

Chapter 1

Degrees of Pedigrees

READERS' PRE-TEST

As a rule, psychopaths

a. are handsome (or beautiful) charmers

b. possess an engaging charisma

c. possess the "gift of gab"

d. are without empathy and conscience

e. are deceptive, remorseless, and cold-blooded

f. are, above all, compulsive liars

g. possess no moral compass

h. are behaviorally maladapted, thus creating social disharmony

i. possess sexually perverted brain conditions

j. all of the above

The answer is *j,* all of the above.

As we become more familiar with *psychopathy*—one of the most misunderstood terms in modern society—readers will see the necessity of our *neurospectrum* showing gradations of vigorous brain conditions. The combination of observable behavior and unobservable thoughts and habits hidden in the perverted motivations of corruptive and/or violent psychopaths requires that all of the answers listed above be true. The "auditions" of psychopaths are indeed deceptive, as their "dirty tricks," bordering on

Oscar-winning performances, come to the forefront when victims are introduced to the Mr. Hyde side of these people. Although most run-of-the-mill criminals (usually larcenous antisocial types) are not psychopaths, they still may display evidence of psychopathic characteristics of the kind described in this chapter's profile of Ottis Toole.

In this volume, we address the differences and similarities of psychopathic characteristics, whether they are passionate and socially acceptable as observed in society's movers and shakers or, in extreme variations, whether behavior can be correctly called "psychopathic." In worst-case scenarios, would prey be introduced to "Mr. Hyde" in pathological (violent) psychopaths? The rise of neuroscience, particularly neuropsychology, over the past two decades has provided forensic investigative scientists with valuable information far beyond what had earlier been known about violent sexual perpetrators. Now even the general public, many of whom enjoy TV shows featuring crime-scene investigations, can understand criminal minds as maladapted brains responsible for corruption and violence, particularly psychopathic sexual violence related to serial crime. Psychopathy does not necessarily refer to maladaptive and criminal varieties alone, in fact, moderate psychopathic traits can be life-affirming and define passionate achievers, as indicated in the quote below.

Psychopaths are fearless, confident, charismatic, ruthless, and focused. Yet contrary to popular belief, they are not necessarily violent. Far from its being an open and shut case—you're either a psychopath or you're not—there are, instead, inner and outer zones of the disorder . . . there is a spectrum of psychopathy along which each of us has our place, with only a small minority of A-listers resident in the "inner city." (Dutton 2012, 11)

We maintain throughout this volume that focusing on vigorous brain conditions or *brainmarks* (marks of chemical connections and transitions known to drive behavior) will produce evidence of behavioral red flags. All too often, red flags are ignored—for a variety of reasons soon to be addressed.

The perennial question addressed in sexual forensics is this: How beneficial would a warning of "likely behaviors" be to the female brain "wired" from birth to be attracted to, and ultimately trust, handsome and charming males possessing the gift of gab? We argue that red flags providing vital clues to real identities can be made effective to the female brain. Vigorously deceptive criminals offer visible clues that have been routinely ignored. As even Charles Darwin noted in regard to deceptive males, "The most vigorous individuals, those which have most successfully struggled with their conditions of life, will generally leave most progeny. But success will often depend on having special weapons or means of defense, or on the charms of males; and the slightest advantage will lead to victory" (Darwin 2009).

ADAPTIVE NEUROPLASTICITY

Adaptation to the everyday challenges of life, including sexual behavior, is driven by vigorous brain conditions created by degrees of pedigrees (expectancies anticipated from genetics/gene pools or ancestry) from ancient survival scripts. This is another way of saying our cortical "wiring" has served us well over millennia, with gradual changes required to meet physical and social environmental challenges. Our species sits atop the food chain because we have adapted successfully to all the "slings and arrows" thrown our way, allowing us to survive and thrive. Today, we know why: The brain is a natural organ of adaptation, embracing change due to its biologically mandated abilities to rewire and reconfigure its cortical structures. This inherent ability has a name: *adaptive neuroplasticity.* This dynamic cortical changeability has enabled our species to overcome dangerous addictions, obsessions, and compulsions. Combined with this cortical changeability are our brainmarks, the powerful cascading biochemistry driving the production of progeny in sexual passions. In other words, we are good at adapting to changes needed in sexual pursuits to create progeny and further the species.

The need to procure sex is a constant in our lives from puberty onward. Orchestrating sexual pleasure is one of the brain's most enduring qualities; unfortunately, when perversion twists and mangles this ancient pedigree, sexual abuse and violence produce toxic sexuality, destroying lives. In this chapter, we provide examples of sexualized perversions through real crimes perpetrated by antisocial criminals as well as psychopathic serial killers.

> *"Kar, wake up," he said, shaking her. She opened her eyes slowly to see his face flushed and his eyes dancing with excitement.*
>
> *"I did it," he said, sounding like a schoolboy who has passed an exam. "I got a girl. She's in the house, downstairs."*
>
> *Homolka thought, at first, that he had picked up a woman at a bar. She didn't want to believe he had done as he promised and kidnapped a woman. . . .*
>
> *Although it was after 3 a.m. Bernardo was acting as if it was midafternoon. This was his time of the day, when he was most aroused. Though Leslie was sobbing, asking him to let her go, it wasn't going*

to do her any good. He had waited a long time to get his very own sex
slave, and he had no intention of depriving himself of the pleasure. He
was going to take his time with her.

(Pron 1995)

SEXUAL ADAPTATION VERSUS MALADAPTATION

In the struggle for existence, individuals who adapt successfully to challenges thrown their way mostly survive. When they choose to live within the civil and criminal laws of society, they opt for a life geared to social harmony, and they may even rise above the masses and become wealthy and influential. Those who choose the criminal pathway often pay heavy fines and/or serve jail time for breaches of the law. Making one bad decision after another, including taking illegal drugs, can produce criminal penalties that severely alter one's quality of life. Most of us strive to live in social harmony by avoiding the unlawful, the corruptive, the illegal, and the violent. But there will always be some who choose not control themselves and thus choose to live with self-entitled arrogance. Below we address the continuum (or in our terminology, the neurospectrum) of the powerful chemistry known to lie behind the behavior we choose, thus producing highly predictable behavior (as neurotruths).

From a neuropsychology perspective, we argue that law-abiding citizens exhibit pedigrees of neurochemical cascades that reinforce adaptive behavior. This powerful chemistry will be addressed in upcoming chapters. After describing various neurochemical characteristics, we will define their efficacy as biochemical architects of behavior. Other than simple reflexes, all behavior comes from the cortical-chemical configuration of our brains.

Our brains are "marked" or primed from birth to produce vigorous brain conditions known to move behavior and affect (feelings and mood). Today we know behavior comes from vigorous brain conditions including psychological deception and other variations of virtues, vulgarities, and corruption common to criminal minds, normal minds, and all minds in between.

PEDIGREES OF LUST EXPRESSED AS PASSION

There is yet another pedigree of individuals around the midline of the spectrum, beyond the elementary survivors and thrivers, who by their chemical pedigrees and behavior apply their passion, motivation, and drive to causes and careers that often become distinguished. Even as children, their predictable indicators of willpower and drive could be observed—they were busy-bee entrepreneurs or wide-eyed dreamers and mavericks. Later, with or without the benefit of higher education, they often rose to great heights through hard work, dedication, and innovation. Examples of such dreamers and mavericks include Steve Jobs, who merged technology with the humanities; Ted Turner, who dreamed of a twenty-four-hour news channel; and Elizabeth Arden, who in the early decades of the 1900s redefined feminine beauty as she methodically opened her Red Door beauty salons. The passionate often change the way the rest of us communicate, our perception of ourselves, and our perception of the world. Such innovators add depth to those who seek compelling lives yet are not themselves innovators or trendsetters.

The range of adaptive versus maladaptive behaviors configured across a spectrum of foundational influences characterizes our modern understanding of human behavior. On this line of pedigrees, we place survivors and thrivers to the far left, passionate achievers toward the midline, and corruptive and antisocial behavior before the extreme far right of pathological psychopaths configuring maladaptive perversions. Behavior manifested to the far right of the midline represents illegal and/or violent behavior leading to corruption and criminal violence, which then lead to social disharmony and chaos. Such offenders must be extracted from society like a "bad tooth" and locked away in warehouses (prisons) for psychopaths and the antisocial.

It is abundantly clear that antisocial criminals are not in the same ballpark as the pedigree of pathological psychopaths. However, they often share some of the same characteristics.

EVERYTHING IS A CLUE: IDENTIFYING TOOLE, BERNARDO, AND HOMOLKA

> *Whatever "reasoning" is ultimately used, choosing violent sexual predation as the way to go—as the way of life—quickly segues into obsession and compulsion for more victims. The entire enterprise pays enormous benefits to the predator—he gets to manipulate, dominate, and control with sexual perversion for as long as he wants, even in her death.*

(Jacobs 2013)

Two real-life examples of typical and long-standing antisocial criminal types (and pathological psychopaths, the stalking killers and rapists who step from the shadows as trapdoor spiders to create horrific crimes) are Ottis Edward Toole and the team of Paul Bernardo and Karla Homolka—Canada's "Ken and Barbie" serial killers.

We start our excursion into criminal minds by recognizing red flags of behavior that should alert us to possible dangers from a person "auditioning" before us. Psychopaths audition differently from antisocial criminals, the latter often larcenists who steal money and property in complicated financial schemes and may have a history of lengthy jail sentences. In contrast, psychopaths adhere to strategic plans of deception often involving stalking to unleash unspeakable violence on unsuspecting prey. Often, their crimes go undetected for years, and in some instances, their gruesome crimes remain forever unsolved "cold cases."

Regardless, understanding red flags can save lives. Does the individual before us have our best interests at heart? Or is there, beneath the "Dr. Jekyll" smiling face, a perverted "Mr. Hyde"?

ANTISOCIAL CRIMINALS

Antisocial criminals break laws for a variety of reasons—to be unjustly enriched, for reckless disregard, just to be mean bullies, or due to a lifestyle of crime learned as children. From Mafia bosses, con men, and gangsters who inspired pulp fiction from the 1920s to 1940s to contemporary street thugs, antisocials who break society's laws and are damn proud of it.

Generally, antisocial criminals are not particularly charming, handsome, or intelligent. Yet they often display "animal cunning," allowing them to become proficient in deception; they construct a persona to lure their victims. In other words, they show Dr. Jekyll while keeping Mr. Hyde hidden until just the right moment.

THE GIFT OF SIGHT AND A FUNCTIONAL AMYGDALA

One only needs the gift of sight and a functional amygdala—the brain's "alarm system," which detects creepy vibes from others—to avoid most antisocial criminals. Strictly speaking, antisocial criminals with accompanying psychopathic traits speak volumes on the complexities of the human condition and create challenges for those in criminal justice trying to apprehend them. Hence, varieties of what we call *differently-abled* brain conditions produce red flags that often go unnoticed. Consider the case of former Pennsylvania State University football coach Jerry Sandusky, who showed the world his Dr. Jekyll side (the respectable side) while privately, to his sexual prey, he showed his Mr. Hyde side. Such deception happens too often, as recently observed in the scandals of former University of Arkansas coach Bobby Petrino and much earlier seen in the career of Dave Bliss, the college basketball coach who portrayed one of his players as a drug dealer in order to escape a closer examination of his own actions. There are examples beyond coaching, of course, reaching into the world of corrupt CEOs, politicians, and others.

Severe mental issues and toxic parenting, including severe mental, physical, and sexual abuses, as well as disengaged parenting, which engenders situations in which children are routinely ignored and devalued, can combine to create a maladapted person headed for a life of antisocial crime. When addiction is added to this scenario, matters only get worse.

Clinically speaking, "diagnosis" of a criminal type is not always as simple as following categorically a list of so-called diagnostic criteria. For instance, the case of Ottis Toole, an antisocial criminal whose early formative experiences delivered massive doses of toxicity from a variety of sources—familial red flags—exists as a prime example of a differently-abled antisocial criminal type who possessed, concomitantly, various psychopathic features.

> *It is my belief, based upon several decades of experience, study, and analysis, that the overwhelming majority of repeat sexual offenders do what they do because they want to, because it gives them satisfaction they do not achieve in any other aspect of their lives, and because it makes them feel good, regardless of the consequences to others. In that respect, the crime represents the ultimate in selfishness; the predator doesn't care what happens to the victim as long as he gets what he wants.*

(Douglas 1998, 33–34)

It is my belief, based upon almost three decades of research into adolescent and young adult brains and behavior, plus more than ten years of independent research into criminal minds, that the word *selfishness* is not a strong enough word to convey the state of a sexually maladapted brain in this age of neuroscience. Indeed, predatory crimes of financial corruption and larceny suggest arrogance or pathological selfishness. Furthermore, violent crimes such as rape and homicide display an even more perverted variation of arrogance—grandiose arrogance—the variety required to destroy life.

The following profiles of differently-abled criminals contrast the perversions often observed in antisocial criminal types versus psychopathic serial killer types. We begin with Ottis Elwood Toole, who displays a few psychopathic traits cocooned within strong antisocial characteristics. He was not handsome, charming, or gifted with the ability to smooth talk, but he was deceptive and adept at using any ruse that would blindside his prey.

MAKING THE CASE FOR THE DIFFERENTLY-ABLED I: OTTIS ELWOOD TOOLE (1947–1996)

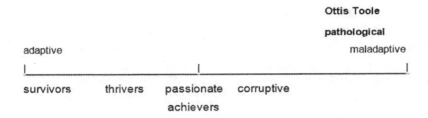

First I go out and catch me a little boy, maybe go down to a mall or shopping center and grab one there . . . grab him, tie him up, use a gag, put him in the trunk of my car and drive him to my place out in the swamps. Nobody to bother me way out there.

Ottis Elwood Toole

An American serial killer and arsonist, Ottis Toole gained infamy from his role as an accomplice of convicted serial killer Henry Lee Lucas. On December 16, 2008, Toole was identified as having murdered and decapitated Adam Walsh, the son of John Walsh, creator of the television series *America's Most Wanted,* which profiles criminals in order to assist law enforcement in capturing fugitives.

Also known as the "Jacksonville Cannibal," Toole was born and raised in Jacksonville, Florida, by a religiously fanatical mother and an alcoholic father who soon abandoned the family. By Toole's own accounts, he was abused by his mother and forced by his sister to wear girl's clothing and play as "Becky." Toole's maternal grandmother was a Satanist who often referred to him as the "devil's child" and exposed him to such behaviors as self-mutilation, grave robbing, and making magical charms out of stolen body parts. At the tender age of 5, Toole was forced to have sex with a friend of his father's. By the age of 10, he considered himself a homosexual, and he developed a sexual relationship with a neighborhood boy by the time he was 12 years old. Toole dropped out of school in the ninth grade and started hanging out in local gay bars. He was known to dress in drag and participate in male prostitution.

With an IQ of 75, Toole is believed to have suffered from mild mental retardation as well as attention deficit hyperactivity disorder (ADHD), dyslexia, epilepsy, illiteracy, and, some experts suggest, paranoid schizophrenia. A frequent runaway, he often slept in abandoned houses.

Sexually aroused by fire, Toole evolved into a serial arsonist, torching vacant houses in the neighborhood because he "hated to see them standing there."

After being propositioned for sex by a traveling salesman, Toole drove over the salesman with the man's car, committing his first murder at the age of 14. Between 1966 and 1973, Toole drifted around the southwestern United States, supporting himself with prostitution and panhandling. In 1974, he was a prime suspect in both the Nebraska murder of 24-year-old Patricia Webb and the Colorado killing of 31-year-old Ellen Holman. Toole hitchhiked back to Jacksonville to escape the allegations and later married a women 25 years his senior. When she learned of his homosexuality, she left him. They had been married for three days.

While in a prison soup kitchen in 1976, Toole met Henry Lee Lucas, and the two quickly formed a sexual relationship. Toole later admitted to accompanying Lucas while the latter committed 108 murders under the influence of a cult called the Hands of Death, headquartered on a Mexican ranch. Along with other cult members, Toole would sacrifice children and virgins picked up while hitchhiking, sitting in bars, or just walking down the road near the Texas-Mexico border. During secret cult rituals, the victims were placed on an altar and their throats were cut. Their blood was then collected, placed in a goblet, and passed around for all to drink. Sexual organs were also removed and cooked according to recipes. Altogether, Toole claimed that he and Lucas murdered more than 200 women, men, boys and girls across 11 states.

Though Toole preferred male victims, he was not opposed to females, favoring anal penetration, strangulation, shooting, and slicing their throats. After some sexual encounters, Toole admitted to eviscerating his victims and roasting their corpses on a spit; he even bragged about making his own barbeque sauce for such occasions. In early 1981, Toole suffered the deaths of both his mother and sister. In July of that same year, six-year-old Adam Walsh went missing from a mall in Hollywood, Florida. Adam's head was found in August near a canal at Vero Beach, but his body was never recovered. Two years later, Toole would voice a deathbed confession to this heinous crime.

Toole received his first death sentence for the 1982 murder of 64-year-old George Sonnenberg, who was locked in his home, which was then set on fire. His second death sentence came for shooting 19-year-old Ada Johnson in the head after picking her up at a Tallahassee nightclub. Both death sentences were later appealed and commuted to life. Toole pleaded guilty to four additional murders and received four more life sentences. "I got off death row because they said I'm too sick to burn on the electric chair," Toole claimed, adding, "People eat pigs, cows, and horses. I like to eat people. It's good meat, too. You ain't tried it, don't be saying it ain't tasty. You might like it" (Barton 1996).

On September 15, 1986, at the age of forty-nine, Toole died of liver failure in his prison cell. Unclaimed by family members, his body was later buried in a prison cemetery.

PEDIGREE OF PSYCHOPATHIC CHARACTERISTICS

America has become a nation known for "psychopathic characteristics" fueled by the lack of a moral compass. We have to look no further than the top ten models of arrogance in our country to see the shape we're in: politics, Congress, big business, banks, CEOs, celebrities, professional sports, big pharmaceutical companies, pop culture, and social networking. They are hives for arrogance and deception.

Criminally violent psychopaths, defined using criteria from the Hare Psychopathy Checklist-Revised (PCL-R) (Hare 2003), possess the following pedigrees: they are superficially charming, they are "lookers" (males are often handsome and females are beautiful) who display a glib affect (meaning they are experts at mixing adaptability with deception), they are cunning and manipulative, and they are trapdoor spiders, able to blindside their unsuspecting prey, who never see the true monster beneath the surface until it's too late.

How could so much harm come from so much charm? In this ultimate version of pathological psychopathy, *aggressive narcissism* (Factor 1 of the PCL-R) is described as displaying the following characteristics:

- A grandiose sense of self-worth (we prefer the term *grandiose arrogance*)
- Pathological lying
- A lack of remorse or guilt
- A shallowness of affect (superficial emotional affect absent genuine concern)
- A lack of empathy
- A failure to accept responsibility for one's own behavior
- Promiscuous sexual behavior

A *socially deviant* lifestyle—PCL-R Factor 2—encompasses a propensity for boredom, which necessitates constant stimulation, as well as a parasitic lifestyle enhanced by poor behavioral controls. Factor 2's social deviance is also demonstrated by a lack of realistic long-term goals, impulsivity, irresponsibility, and instances of juvenile delinquency. Another key factor in severe psychopathy is the expression of criminal versatility—larceny as well as sexual predation.

Able to appear as though they possess high levels of intelligence, and to participate in various criminal schemes, severe psychopaths will commit any number of lesser crimes in order to experience the "emotional highs" that are the focus of their ongoing cognitive perversion. Such was seen in the case of Paul Bernardo and Karla Homolka.

MAKING THE CASE FOR THE DIFFERENTLY-ABLED II: PAUL BERNARDO (1964–) AND KARLA HOMOLKA (1970–)

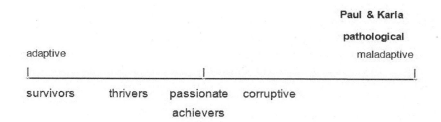

When dressed in his Boy Scout uniform, Paul Bernardo, the cute little kid with the sweet smile, dimpled cheeks, and blond hair, looked like the boy every parent wanted. But he would grow up to be the "Scarborough Rapist" (1987–91) and, along with Karla Homolka, the driving force behind Canada's most prolific serial killer team.

In 1987, when she was 17 years old, Karla Homolka met Paul Bernardo, then age 23, in a restaurant while both were attending a conference in Toronto. The lethal relationship was christened by sex within hours. Paul ran a cigarette-smuggling scheme while he worked by day as an accountant. After graduating from high school, Karla worked as an assistant in a pet store, where she stole the drugs used to render victims unconscious during the violent assaults the couple committed by night. The killers' favored modus operandi (MO) was to drug their victims before sexually assaulting them in a violent manner—which eventually led to the deaths of victims Leslie Mahaffy and Kristen French, for example. Mahaffy's body was dismembered and encased in cement blocks that were thrown overboard into Lake Gibson.

The body count rose as the violent and sadistic crimes of Bernardo and Homolka continued. Author Nick Pron wrote a compelling account of the crimes in his book, *Lethal Marriage* (1995), and the pair's crimes were documented by the film *Karla* (2004), which gave visual testament to the horrific actions of the couple.

Karla Homolka, a blond beauty, negotiated a plea bargain with authorities when the couple was first arrested. Public outrage followed the deal, which put Bernardo in prison (where he remains today) and reduced Karla's sentence to 12 years because she claimed Bernardo forced her by abuse into a life of supporting his rapes and murders, including the death of her own sister, Tammy, a virgin offered by Karla as a wedding present to Paul. Tammy choked on her own vomit, unconscious after being drugged by the couple. (However, a videotape the couple made of the sexual assaults of Tammy Homolka and others later surfaced, showing Karla as an active participant.)

Today, Paul waits in prison for his parole hearing, set for the year 2020. For Karla, who was released from prison on July 4, 2005, it's another story. Canadian investigative journalist and lawyer Paula Todd, the author of *Inside Out,* a book documenting the lives of violent criminals released from prison, tracked Karla, who vanished from Montreal in 2007. She found her on the Caribbean island of Guadeloupe living as Leanne Bordelais, with her three children (a daughter and two sons) and husband, Thierry Bordelais. Todd's investigation was published in June 2012 as Canada's first e-book for breaking news (*Finding Karla: How I Tracked Down an Elusive Serial Child Killer and Discovered a Mother of Three*). Todd admits, "The thing about Karla Homolka and the reasons she persists in Canadians' minds is that she fooled everybody" (*Huffington Post Canada,* June 21, 2012).

THE VERDICT FROM CHAPTER 1

There is a strong indication of emotional engagement connecting powerful regions of our brains in pedigrees of psychopathy not observed in run-of-the-mill antisocial criminals. We are speaking of all pedigrees of powerful chemistry across the neurospectrum, from survivors and thrivers to passionate achievers to the more obvious criminal versions—the corruptive larcenists and headline-grabbing pathological varieties, the two varieties deserving the tag of "psychopath."

To the left of center on the neurospectrum are individuals who are the "salt of the earth," who survive and thrive in their normalcy. Further right are those who are passionate achievers, such as Steve Jobs and Ted Turner.

A question we can answer only if we know the configuration of female brains is this: Why are most females vulnerable to the charms of handsome males? (This question illustrates neurotruth 4 from my list of eighteen neurologically based facts; see chapter 11 for the full list.) There is a certain *je ne sais quoi*—a quality that's hard to define yet engaging and perhaps a little dangerous—in those from the middle to the far right side of the neurospectrum; such differently-abled pedigrees are perceived as "bad boys."

Visually, psychopaths are frequently stunning. Males are usually alpha males, handsome, sexy, and charming with an engaging manner of speech. Most females become stimulated sexually as soon as these charmers enter a room. To feed their sexually driven appetites, such males never need to physically grab their prey; they do it all with good looks and a gift of gab (in direct contrast to most antisocial criminal types, who often must physically capture their prey with help from a weapon, rope, handcuffs, or an anesthetic-soaked rag).

Chapter 2

Screaming Red Flags

READERS' PRE-TEST

Forensic science research into psychopathy and criminal minds is greatly benefited

a. at the tissue level by understanding vigorous brain conditions
b. by everyday citizens addressing behavioral "red flags"—making visible the invisible
c. by research into violent, incarcerated psychopaths
d. by applying neurotruths from research into traumatized brains
e. all of the above

The answer is *e,* all of the above.

Neurotruths from brain neuroscience (neuropsychology) regarding violent sexuality have been affirmed straight from the mouths of sexual offenders and are described in detail in the FBI's 1978 study of known-offender characteristics (KOC). In the study, offenders shared the motivations and incidentals of motivations that led to their crimes.

Today investigative scientists are able to understand how regions of the brain—such as the paralimbic system—can become maladapted. Thus it is impossible to construct an accurate crime-scene science without advancing brain-scanning knowledge as well as addressing the habits, patterns, and formative influences that have shaped and maintained the sexually violent minds of pathological psychopaths. Former FBI agents Robert Ressler and

John Douglas gave researchers a model for violent psychopathy in 1978 with their groundbreaking personality profile studies of incarcerated offenders. And one thing they discovered was completely unanticipated: Violent offenders love talking about their crimes. Not just in violence, but in moderation, psychopathic traits are found everywhere in society, especially in those who have passionate careers that call for subtle abilities to handle stress and frustration on the way to making personal fortunes such as:

There are positions in society—jobs and roles to fulfill—which, by their competitive, cutthroat, or chillingly coercive natures, require access to office space precisely the kind of psychological real estate that psychopaths have the keys to, that they have an offer in the glossy neural portfolios. *Given that such roles— predominately by virtue of their inherent stress and danger—often confer great wealth, danger, status, and prestige on the individuals who assume them . . . it's really not surprising that the genes have hung around (in gene pools)* [emphasis added]. (Dutton 2012, 107)

SEX SEALS A LOT OF DEALS

Continuing our thoughts from chapter 1, 17-year-old Karla Homolka chose to have sex with charming and handsome Paul Bernardo, aged 23, one hour after they met at a conference. Sex sealed the deal in their minds, thus launching a relationship that would produce Canada's Ken and Barbie serial killers—the team that caused so much grief to families who lost daughters to these psychopathic killers. Today, Bernardo remains confined in prison, his first chance for parole coming in 2020. As described in chapter 1, Karla was released from prison after serving only four years.

SEXUAL FORENSICS AND FOUNDATIONAL NEUROTRUTHS

Let's get right to the most important neurotruth in preventing becoming a statistic of sexually psychopathic crime. For females, the foundational neurotruth of self-protection is to "shut down" predators before they get a head of steam. As John Douglas (1998, 132–133) notes, "When a predator realizes, after each successive experience, that his fantasy hasn't been completely fulfilled, rather than look for another outlet—a productive and legal one—he gets more frustrated and even angrier. This is why we often see an escalation of violence in an UNSUB's series of crimes. And this is why I say that until a predator is locked up, dies, or grows too old and feeble to commit his crime of choice, he will never stop." Understand the importance of becoming a headstrong, independent woman (or at least appearing to be) with a maturity beyond that of typical teenagers, and of showing these signs in early adolescence and by leaps and bounds in late adolescence into the early twenties. This behavior counteracts the mindset of predators, who expect young prey to be, at best, naïve. A good acting job will turn the tide.

In the predator's one-track mind, a strong female is "just not worth the trouble." Appearing to be strong is a female's first line of defense for alerting his frenzied brain that the woman standing before him is not impressed by charm and cannot be manipulated and controlled. But for this strategy to work, she must be convincing in her part of the "audition" as the predator stands before her. She can't "melt" at his touch; she must be convincingly in control. Again, she will come across as just too much trouble for his pursuit. The red flags of his impatience will show, signaling that all he wants is to use her to satisfy his fantasies—and by resistance, she has won.

There is great utility and self-esteem in being able to control oneself and, in particular, in counteracting faux charm with hardheaded independence— thus avoiding the harm that can come from so much charm. From her due diligence, the strong female can expect the predator's exit from her life, as he forages and auditions for more immature and naïve victims. Such was the case with rapist and serial killer Paul Bernardo: "He was uncomfortable around women with forceful personalities. He had dated one woman for two weeks, never going any further than kissing her, before he broke off the relationship. She was too aggressive for him" (Pron 1995, 62).

FACTS SUPPORT NEUROTRUTHS

In contrast, Karla Homolka only pretended to be feisty and headstrong to her parents. Truth was, she loved having boys grope her and was looking for the right man to give her the sexual thrills of a lifetime: "According to psychiatrists . . . Homolka living in a houseful of women, was looking for a strong man who exuded a sense of dominance. [She] would have found Bernardo's decisive, self-assured and a successful image particularly appealing. She suffered from a sense of insecurity, and with her conciliatory, self-doubting nature, hoped to draw out assurances and directions from a stronger, male partner. . . . It was a perfect match, Homolka believing she needed a forceful man in her life, and Bernardo searching for vulnerable women he could control. But the nature of Bernardo's particular lusts would set it on a course toward murder. . . . He needed a compliant female with whom he could act out all of his oft-criminal sexual fantasies, someone who he could control to the point of life and death over her" (Pron 1995, 62).

Long before he met Karla, and by his midteens, Bernardo was deep into pornography, especially enjoying tapes of bondage and women being raped.

Also, he was an accomplished voyeur and enjoyed a fetish for women posing in their underwear in glossy magazine ads. Ten-year-old girls were just as stimulating to him as pictures of adult women. It is not shocking, therefore, that immersed as he was in sexually stimulating images, he objectified women, turning them into compliant sexual objects. Naturally, he wanted the real thing—a living, breathing woman he could have "kinky sex" with and make his sex slave. When he was 19, he met her, and she was just 16. Lucy (not her real name) was a virgin, sexually naïve, and marginally intelligent (Pron 1995, 50). He sexually abused her for three years, largely in his car behind a factory in a deserted parking lot. Gone was his sweet smile and delicate voice (ibid.). As one might surmise, Lucy kept secret all of his horrific sexual abuses. She did not want her parents to know. Finally, she managed to break off the relationship. Yet the worst was still to come for innocent victims who would face Bernardo's sexual perversion. He was about to meet the woman of his dreams, Karla Homolka.

What the general public, police, and forensic investigative scientists can learn from Bernardo and Homolka is the ease by which sexual predators can fool everyone. Crown prosecutor Greg Barnett would eventually state in pretrial arguments that Bernardo started to develop his theme of "Deadly Innocence" as a teenager. "He gave the impression of being a pretty boy, but underneath he's full of violence . . . willing to kill," Barnett stated. "It's the projection of the image of deception" (Pron 1995, 55–56). Ironically, some of the people who badly misjudged Bernardo would be police officers, their suspicions sidetracked by his soft looks and polite manner. Others would be women fatally drawn to his soft smile and deadly charm, not realizing until it was too late how dangerous he was (ibid.).

Theodore "Ted" Bundy is one of the most recognizable of all serial killers. His crimes have been well documented by investigative scientists and investigative journalists. What follows is an analysis of Bundy's crimes.

MAKING THE CASE FOR THE DIFFERENTLY-ABLED I: THEODORE "TED" BUNDY (1946–1989)

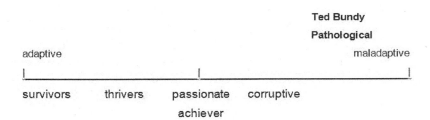

Ted was lucky, but he was also supremely capable, an almost perfect killing machine who struck with the poise and art of a born
predator. His genius was to know when to kill and where to kill,
knowledge that was his by instinct and by dint of careful study of
his craft.

Stephen Michaud (Aynesworth 1999)

Theodore Robert Cowell was born in a home for unwed mothers. His
mother was Louise Cowell, and his father's identity was unknown. Louise
claimed she was seduced by a sailor, yet some family members contend
her own father, a violent and abusive man, might have committed incest.
Ted was raised by his maternal grandparents, who posed as his real parents while mother Louise became his "sister" to avoid the social stigma of
illegitimacy at that time.

Ted would grow up to become one of the most sadomasochistic serial
killers and necrophiliacs in American history. Shortly before his execution
in 1989, he confessed to 30 homicides across seven states; however, the
dates and number of killings are still in dispute. Likely there were more
than 30.

Nothing was more exciting to him then reading about sexually abusing
females. He boasted his prey were pretty but naïve.

Stephen Michaud (Aynesworth 1999)

Charming, charismatic, and easy talking, Bundy chose victims with an
appearance similar to that of his college sweetheart. With his arm in a
make-believe sling, feigning injury, he would ask a young woman to help
him carry his books across campus to his car. At other times, he imper-
sonated authority figures such as police officers. As a psychology major,
he graduated from the University of Washington in 1972 and briefly
attended law school.

By his own admission, from an early age he was addicted to hard-
core pornography and soon became a functional alcoholic. In 1974,
when he was 27, he committed his earliest documented murders, but
it is possible his first murder occurred when he was fourteen and that
his victim was an 8-year-old girl. In 1981, he volunteered to work for
Seattle's suicide hotline and worked in the same room with former
police officer and aspiring true-crime writer Ann Rule; she saw nothing
alarming or disturbing in his demeanor, later referring to Bundy as
kind, solicitous, and empathetic in her book *The Stranger Beside Me*
(Signet, 1980).

In some instances, Bundy revisited crime scenes and applied
makeup he had applied to the faces of the decomposing corpses and

then committed acts of necrophilia. He decapitated some of his victims and kept the severed heads in his apartment as souvenirs. Other times, he broke into sorority houses or apartments after midnight and bludgeoned victims as they slept. He once referred to himself as "the most cold-hearted son of a bitch you'll ever meet" (Aynesworth 1999). In many ways, Bundy is the poster predator for the organized serial killer of FBI typology: He stalked his prey until he could attack or simply broke into apartments in anger after not finding those he had stalked at home.

Bundy believed he was a victim himself—of incompetent defense attorneys, poisonous pretrial publicity, and manipulated evidence: "I was caught in a monstrous tangle of circumstance that led me from a life of promise and public spirit to unjust prosecution, imprisonment, and three death sentences. I am innocent" (Aynesworth 1999).

According to Michaud (Aynesworth 1999), Bundy was his "own abstraction, a lethal absurdity masquerading as a man." When asked how his crimes all started, Bundy saw himself as an illegitimate child of his times, teased and exploited. He told Michaud that long before the overpowering need to kill, he had juvenile fantasies fed by photos of women in magazines, women in ads for suntan products, and even "jiggly" starlets on TV talk shows. Crime stories fascinated him. He read detective magazines and gradually gained knowledge about criminal techniques—what worked and what did not. However, nothing was more exciting to him than reading about the sexual abuse of females. Nevertheless, he was training himself. Alcohol was a potent part of the game, a spur to go hunting, just as it was for shoplifting, a parallel avocation. Speaking of himself as though he were another person, he claimed, "I think you could make a little more sense out of much of this if you take into account the effect of alcohol. It's important. It's very important as a trigger. When this person drank a good deal, his inhibitions were significantly diminished. He would find that his urge to engage in voyeuristic behavior, or trips to the bookstore [pornography], would be more prevalent, more urgent. It was as though the dominant personality was sedated. On every occasion he engaged in such behavior, he was intoxicated" (Aynesworth 1999).

Two months after his 42nd birthday, in 1989, Theodore Cowell was put to death by 2,000 volts of current sent into his copper-lined skullcap, flashing through his body, and down to the ground cable attached to his right leg. His fists clinched once, then again, and then there was no further discernible movement. He was pronounced dead. A female guard had flipped the switch.

MAKING THE CASE FOR THE DIFFERENTLY-ABLED II: JERRY SANDUSKY (1944–)

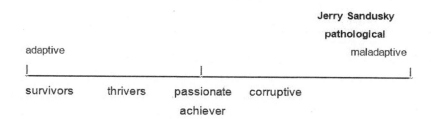

In late June 2012, as the jury began deliberations in the Jerry Sandusky criminal trial, one of his adopted sons, Matt Sandusky, disclosed through his attorney that Sandusky had sexually abused him.

Jerry Sandusky began his career as an assistant football coach at Pennsylvania State University under legendary head coach Joe Paterno in 1969, eventually becoming defensive coordinator in 1977, a position he held until his retirement in 1999. In 1977, Sandusky founded the Second Mile, a nonprofit charity serving Pennsylvania underprivileged and at-risk youth. As it turned out, the sexual grooming began there in what would become one of the most blatant misuses of a charity ever recorded.

In 2011, Sandusky was arrested and charged with 52 counts of sexual abuse of young boys occurring over a 15-year period. His arrest followed a 2-year grand jury investigation, originally with 52 counts but reduced to 48 as the trial opened. In a Harrisburg newspaper in 2012, Sandusky portrayed himself as "someone who would consistently take risks in pursuit of what often is referred to as 'mischief'" (*Patriot-News* 2011). Judging by news photographs showing Sandusky arriving at and leaving the courthouse, his inappropriate affect—emotions such as smiling at inappropriate times and occasionally an apparent lack of emotion—seems to be evidence of neurological damage, most likely some long-standing brain damage the likes of which came to national attention in the filicide murders committed by Susan Smith in 1994.

During Sandusky's trial, prosecutors presented detailed testimony from many of his alleged victims, who recounted explicit sexual acts pressed upon them by Sandusky. The defense, on the other hand, largely built their case upon an oddball strategy—a clinical diagnosis of histrionic personality disorder (HPD), a personality dysfunction inspired by the *Diagnostic and Statistical Manual of Mental Disorders* (DSM) and usually attributed to sexually flirtatious females who use others for money and influence by employing sexually provocative behavior to draw attention to themselves. Nonetheless, shortly before 10:00 p.m. Central Standard Time, breaking news announced that the Sandusky jury returned a verdict of guilty in 45 of the 48 counts of sexual abuse of children.

NEUROTRUTHS EVIDENT IN SEXUAL FORENSICS

Thus far, chapter 2 has provided readers with heads-up alerts regarding the first two red flag–strength neurotruths needed in order to steer clear of harm's way. These neurotruths are directed toward the safety of females, emphasizing the importance of becoming a headstrong, independent woman (or at least appearing to be) with a maturity beyond the typical teenager.

Sexual perversion does not spring forth unannounced, or from the fact that puberty is in full flower, as most males live with a hair trigger of sexual interest in the brain from puberty into middle age and beyond. But most never become rapists or murderers. Rather, sexual perversion has a developmental history stretching all the way back to pre-pubescence. The litany of red flags include addiction to pornography, substance abuse, obsession with sexual fantasies, and sadism—all of which Bundy kept private. The truth is, every single sexual predator has had a red-checkered history, with red flags often going unnoticed or hidden from detection, such as when "troubled" children are home-schooled as parents wrongly attempt to shield maladaptation. This strategy is like attempting to contain lightning in a bottle.

Therefore, sexual crimes stem from earlier sexual obsessions, largely from pornography, voyeurism, exposing oneself, or making sexually explicit phone calls. The crimes that crime-scene investigators study in sexual forensics often began in a harmless enough way, with intensive erotic thoughts that escalated over time to minor, rather than major, brushes with law enforcement. That is, as a first crime, without a developmental history of red flags, no violent criminal wakes up one morning and decides to rape and murder victims as his first offense—just as Bundy graduated from voyeurism to larceny, then to sexually explicit phone calls, and then to stalking. In other cases of sexually psychopathic serial crimes, early experiences involving cruelty to pets and setting fires have been uncovered. Criminal background checks that almost anyone can "run" these days is an easy way to discover and accumulate facts about others that may be thoroughly shocking.

Neurotruth number 3 comes as a bundled assortment of characteristics found in the backgrounds of offenders and their families. These characteristics, gathered from the FBI's Criminal Personality Research Profile, a fifty-seven-page questionnaire of thirty-six incarcerated serial killers in the 1970s, have known neuro-influences affecting vigorous brain conditions. Of the characteristics obtained from the FBI questionnaire (Douglas et al. 1992), it is evident by today's standards that many have known biological underpinnings, and the remainder are heavily influenced by both nature (biology) and nurture (social learning)—especially toxic parenting in highly dysfunctional family milieus, which is known to have a significant impact on brain development (such dysfunction and toxicity is equivalent to being hit in the head repeatedly). Few general readers have even heard of such a list of characteristics, much less studied it, so we include it here. According to Ressler (1992), 100 percent of perpetrators of sexual crimes experienced the following:

- Sexual dysfunction to the point of being unable to sustain a mature, consensual relationship with another person
- Serious emotional, mental, or physical abuse
- Being ignored (due to disengaged parenting) so that no limits were imposed on their behavior
- No significant familial attachment, resulting in feeling "lonely and isolated"
- "Negative and destructive influences" between the ages of eight and twelve (no strong, influential adult rescued any of them)
- Atypical sexual development to the point that they were sexually dysfunctional
- Being consumed by negative outlets—drugs, vandalism, burglary, and pornography—as no positive stimulation existed
- Perverse sexual fantasies that fueled murderous acts
- Compulsive and perverted sexual fantasies that resulted in brutalizing sexual forensics at crime scenes (where victims were depersonalized as though "evicted from their bodies," as one killer described it)
- Sexual obsession that caused them to become disconnected from affection and tender emotions
- Deviant and sexualized "cognitive maps" that stimulated perversity that pornography only temporarily satisfied, "forcing" offenders to confront live victims
- So-called pre-crime triggers—some perception of a loss: a job, money problems, a vociferous argument, or the "brutal urge" for another victim

Between 50 and 75 percent of these perpetrators experienced the following:

- Mental illness in immediate families
- Family members involved in some form of criminality

- A family history of alcohol or drug abuse
- Maternal bonding (from birth to age seven) with mothers who were uniformly cool, distant, unloving, and neglectful
- Participating in or witnessing sexually stressful events when young (such sexual abuse, attempted rape, or rape)
- Emotional vacancy from being fatherless their adolescent years due to absence (abandonment, divorce), incarceration, or death
- Autoerotic fantasies as preadolescents and rape fantasies between the ages twelve and fourteen
- Compulsive masturbation, lying, enuresis (bed-wetting), and nightmares
- Low academic performance in school (most hated school)

Chapter 3

Sexual Forensics and the Modern Neurospectrum

READERS' PRE-TEST

A neurospectrum shows

a. neurological gradations in strength of chemistry
b. neurological variations in combinations of chemistry
c. the efficacy of hormones
d. the efficacy of neuroglia
e. the efficacy of "gut" probiotics
f. all of the above

The answer is *f*, all of the above.

THE MODERN SPECTRUM BECOMES "NEURO"

As we have noted, spectrums are necessary in the behavioral sciences, including our focus on behavioral neuropsychology—the neuroscience behind how individuals of our species become differently-abled due to vigorous brain conditions and social learning variables. Powerful brain chemistry from neurons and neuroglia produces gradations, variations, and varieties of behavior and affect. When paired with *neurocognitive mapping*—powerful "thinking maps" of behavior enhanced by one's own unique perceptions from individual learning within the family and one's peer milieu—it's no wonder that the differently-abled populate and re-populate our species.

The prefix *neuro-* reflects a hard science pedigree when appended to form words such as *neurology, neuroscience,* and *neuropsychology.* The neurospectrum fits like a glove into our adaptation model—the perspective throughout our book—which is reinforced by over two decades of neuro-science in research labs defining how the central nervous system (CNS)

The Modern Neurospectrum (Jacobs 2011)

The Spectrum is "NEURO" because of the effects of powerful endogenous chemistry and "SPECTRUM" due to gradations of affect and behavior driven by genetics and idiosyncratic experiences observed in adaptive and maladaptive variations.

tenacious & resilient   passionate   arrogance   grandiose arrogance

_____/_____/_____

Survivors	Passionate Achievers	Corruptive /	Pathological
	Muhammad Ali	Rod Blagojevich	
A to Z	Elizabeth Arden	Lance Armstrong	Paul Bernardo
	Sara Blakely Bill Clinton		Karla Homolka
	Jennifer Bricker Richard Nixon		
	Elena Delle Donne		
	Helen Gurley-Brown		
	Truman Capote	Bernard Madoff	
	Jaycee Lee Dugard	Jerry Sandusky	
	Dick Fosbury		Ottis Toole
	Steve Jobs		
	Eliot Ness		
	Kim Peek		
	Mary Shelley		
	"Sully" Sullenberger		
	Ted Turner		

ADAPTIVE--------------------------------/----------------------MALADAPTIVE

70 to 80%   **20 to 30%**

Purposed ranges in evolutionary fitness across the modern neurospectrum

has an impact on behavior and how the CNS is affected by both endogenous (inside our bodies) chemistry and exogenous influences such as drug use and one's parents and peers. More important, perhaps, this perspective provides compelling evidence for ancient survival scripts underlying the modern evolution of our sapient brains.

At stake in our book is a redefinition and a new paradigmatic rendering of *psychopathy*—a term that has been used correctly (and incorrectly) in light of 21st-century neuroscience. As Robert Hare notes in Jon Ronson's *Psychopath Test*, "All the research indicates they [psychopaths] are not a different species . . . they're dimensional. It's a convenience [in defining psychopathy]. If we talk of someone with high blood pressure we talk of them as hypertensives; it's a *term*. . . . Saying 'psychopathic' is like saying 'hypertensive.' . . . And this is what I mean by psychopathy: I mean a score in the upper range of the PCL-R. I'm not sure how high it has to be. For research, thirty is convenient, but it's not absolute" (2011, 268).

In this chapter, we straighten out the "crooked nails" of old-school psychiatry and clinical psychology, which remain contrary to the modern understanding of psychopathy. We must move beyond "personality disorders" to what psychopathy truly is—a vigorous brain condition. This centerpiece of affect, cognition, "personalities," and behavior is the result of powerful brain conditions that define our species as worthy to sit atop the food chain.

In writing this chapter, we envisioned readers as students sitting in our classrooms asking questions about 21st-century psychopathy. At Weatherford College in Weatherford, Texas, we teach two courses addressing psychopathy, Psychology of Adjustment (PSYC 2315) and Introduction to Forensic Psychology (FORS 2450)—both, in our view, absolutely necessary to the preparation of the next generation of forensic investigative scientists. This volume should be a cutting-edge adoption choice for college and university professors who teach courses relative to understanding the neuroscience behind psychopathy and the entire neurospectrum of behavior.

THE FAR RIGHT OF THE SPECTRUM AND CLINICAL CONFUSION

Referring to the modern neurospectrum chart above, let's start at the far right of the spectrum, the place where the best behavioral scientists and researchers in the world crafted the maladaptation of psychopathy with criteria measurable by Hare's Psychopathy Checklist-Revised. In our adaptive perspective, psychopathy is not a disorder so much as it is a maladaptation with corruptive and pathological consequences; such outcomes result in social disharmony (such as compulsive lying and larceny in corruptive versions).

Prior to the impact of the PCL-R and insights from neuropsychology and neuroscans, it was impossible to be clinically diagnosed as a psychopath. The DSM has never published clinical criteria for psychopathy. Here comes clinical confusion. What is antisocial personality disorder? It is the same or similar to psychopathy? What is sociopathy? More confusion. To add fuel to the flames, the word *psychopathy* is not mentioned in the extensive glossary of DSM-IV-TR (the fourth edition of the DSM with a "text revision," 2000). This glaring clinical confusion highlights the need for reconsideration of the inaccuracies of so-called personality disorders and other useless terms currently in use, such as *antisocial personality disorder* and *sociopathy*.

Untangling clinical confusion is a daunting task due almost entirely to divergence in perspectives from academic training. For example, clinicians and academics trained in sociology would naturally favor the role of social interactions such as peer and familial influences in shaping "antisocial personality disorders." Yet, is "toxic parenting" alone enough to produce the pedigree of "monsters" that produce sexual forensics at horrific crime scenes? We just don't know. However, the research literature on psychopathy from those trained in forensic neuropsychology favor biological factors by the preponderance of cruelty and perversion evidenced at crime scenes of sexual forensics. What drives one more toward violence than vigorous brain conditions which meshes well with our evolutionary perspective? The brain is the center of the universe for this perspective not "personality disorders," a lingering reminder of old school ego and personality psychology.

Vigorous brain conditions as primary causes of criminal psychopathy continue to move center stage in the developing field of forensic neuropsychology—the technical name for the analysis of "criminal minds." Clearly, sexual predators do not "suffer" for their crimes; rather they feel energized and entitled. Hence, the importance of genetic health from familial "gene pools" will continue to be emphasized to "weed out" negative factors in parents-to-be who may have experienced serious drug addictions and other factors yet to be discovered—factors that nonetheless impact brain "wiring" in progeny and perhaps contributes to the violence that ignites murder, rape, and serial homicide.

Inherent in clinical criteria, the client (or patient) must "suffer" from this debilitating disorder, mixing aggressive narcissism with antisocial behavior (Meloy 2002; Raine and Sanmartin 2001). Just ask psychopaths themselves how much they suffer. In firsthand accounts given to FBI agents over the last four decades, psychopaths are eager to talk about their "artwork" at crime scenes and claim they never suffer. Even in severe maladaptation, psychopaths feel entitled, empowered, and sexual. How is that suffering? How could they feel "disordered"? In addition, they are seldom psychotic. They know exactly what they are doing and they will continue doing it even when they know arrest is imminent.

Forensic neuropsychologists are not summarily confused. Toward the far right of the spectrum is the realm of corruptive psychopaths fond of Ponzi schemes, such as larcenists Bernard "Bernie" Madoff and Allen Stanford. Corruptive behavior is also noted in those who are compulsive liars, as they often corrupt social harmony; with all the accomplishments of President Clinton and President Nixon, they were both accused of lying and "dirty tricks" while in office.

Violent serial psychopaths do not suffer even when captured, often smiling for the camera. Here's a neurotruth: Arrogance and grandiose arrogance prevent the emotion of suffering. All told, the rapacious pursuit of targeted prey is exciting to psychopaths.

Though psychopaths display *obsessive-compulsive behavior* (OCB) to the sheer delight of their focus and motivation, just like all successful individuals across the normal expanse of 70–80 percent of the spectrum, a glaring difference exists: Psychopaths display *maladaptive perversions* of OCB with deceptive and corruptive illegality or, in severity, with hypersexual and hyperviolent appetites; no known obstacle, except imprisonment without the possibility of parole or a death sentence, prevents the continuation of such violence in pathological varieties. In other words, this severe maladaptation to the far right of the spectrum is irreversible. As Stanton Samenow, coauthor of *Inside the Criminal Mind* (Crown, 1984), an early contribution to understanding criminal minds, asks us, How can individuals who have never been habilitated become rehabilitated?

Are evolutionary designs driving this condition, even though it appears psychopathy is counterproductive to repopulation of the species? A possible answer is just as shocking as the behavior it likely produces. Might this maladaptation function to "thin the herds" in human populations, since the "struggle for existence" must factor in limited resources that indicate not everyone can survive? The truth is that serial killers have always existed. Why? Because we have always had a version of our current brain—a brain that prior to industrialization was likely more violently predatory due to the harsh realities of survival in more austere times.

THINKING OUT LOUD

At this point in our discussion, we resort to thinking out loud: making general statements to readers that represent intellectual food for thought. What vigorous brain conditions seem the most prevalent in driving the pathological psychopathy lying behind the violent psychopaths of the world? At the extreme far right of the spectrum reside irreversible perversion and violence perpetrated by *intraspecies predators* (Hare 1993) who masterfully use deception to lure prey into the predators' comfort zones (trapdoors). Recently, in *Violence and Psychopathy* (Raine and Sanmartin 2001), fresh and convincing evidence for the maladaptive function of the frontal lobes, especially the prefrontal cortex (PFC), of criminally violent psychopaths was presented via positron emission tomography (PET) scans. Under normal conditions, active blood flow and glucose consumption in this neural region is visualized on the scan in bright, warm colors—reds and yellows. Often, however, psychopaths' frontal lobes produced images with "cool-coded" colors—light blues—indicative of diminished blood flow (and thereby activity), which proved to be the standard for maladaptive brain conditions.

THE NEUROSCIENCE OF ARROGANCE

John Douglas and Robert Ressler, retired FBI special agents, extended the validity of criminal psychopathy by gathering known-offender characteristics, an early and courageous instance of forensic investigative science. The hyperviolent and hypersexual behaviors harbored in criminal minds were unearthed via a questionnaire given to known offenders, who surprised the agents by eagerly embracing the opportunity to talk, even to the point of disclosing violent details. Their vicious physical behavior and accompanying fertile erotic imaginations materialized in the questionnaires as the arrogant disregard for human life.

Every scientific paradigm studying vigorous brain conditions views things from a slightly different light, and our perspective is no exception. In our view of the far right of the spectrum, therefore, there exist two gradations of maladaptation—the corruptive and the pathological—producing disruptive and violent behaviors that do not contribute to social harmony. Corruptors engage in illegal schemes and, when caught, are adjudicated by courts of law, while with pathological varieties, prey lose their lives at horrific crime scenes, thus producing sexual forensics.

Like many colleagues, we suspect nature via nurture has scattered behavioral red flags throughout the lives of corruptive charmers and pathological harmers, but it is likely that few interventions were attempted (not that they would have made a difference). To the spectrum's extreme right, serial killers such as Jeffrey Dahmer and Ted Bundy displayed maladapted sexual obsessions and compulsions mixed with violence in perverted erotic imaginations. For his first murder, Dahmer hid in the bushes to knock out a jogger he believed would be passing by, but fortuitously, the jogger had decided not to run that day. Later, Dahmer procured a clothing store mannequin to masturbate upon until he could capture the real thing. Bundy feigned injury to lure unsuspecting coeds on college campuses into carrying his books to his Volkswagen Beetle, minus the passenger seat— one of his trapdoors. The women were struck from behind by a tire iron and handcuffed to the car's gear shift. Another of his MOs was to break into sorority houses to strangle coeds as they slept. John Wayne Gacy lured young adolescent male runaways he encountered at bus stops by promising them jobs with his construction company—while thirty bodies lay rotting in the dirt beneath the crawl space of his modest home. Albert DeSalvo, the "Boston Strangler," experienced strong sexual urges that for him required immediate sexual release, leading to his MO of impersonating a handyman to gain entry to unsuspecting women's homes.

Intraspecies predators (Hare 1993) present themselves as seemingly nonviolent people who often appear shy and socially awkward at first glance. In fact, people associated with such offenders are generally shocked to learn their true natures. Yet it became apparent after the 1970s KOC study that red flags do indeed litter predators' backgrounds, ranging from such minor infractions as making threatening calls and hangups to, in more brazen crimes, inappropriate sexual encounters that often go unreported. Looking deeper into their lives, investigators found "toxic" episodes of disengaged parenting, perverted fantasies of sex mingled with violence occurring in puberty, and/or neurological traumas to the brain such as physical injuries and severe abuse. It is not unusual to discover alcoholism or other chemical addictions as well.

More than two decades of neuroscience have produced compelling evidence that pathological psychopathy becomes personified by *multicausational scripts* of nature via nurture leading to one final outcome: the creation of corruptive and pathological psychopathic varieties expressed in the actions of serial, spree, and mass murderers.

Fraudulent investors Bernard Madoff, Allen Stanford, and Shalom Weiss are among those on an ever-growing list of accomplished con artists who have "killed" investors' life savings with major financial frauds and corruptive rip-offs. In other examples, parents who appear to be upstanding members of their communities, and sometimes hold themselves out as devoutly religious, can just as well be pathologically jealous of others in private and are consumed by Schadenfreude. They seek retribution in secret by disrupting the harmony in communities through, for example, poison-pen letters and other deceptive shenanigans that display who they really are—hateful and vengeful individuals.

As noted earlier, for all the good he accomplished, President Richard Nixon was forced out of office by his lies and obstruction of justice;

President Bill Clinton was impeached by the U.S. House but survived along party lines in the Senate vote; Rod Blagojevich, the former governor of Illinois, received a prison sentence of 14 years—and on and on the list goes. Knowing straightaway the reputations of many if not most politicians, owing to the deceptive practices of many of them, we are left to wonder why they would seek such a profession. Do they crave the feeling and influence of power? Or do they have glorious intentions mirroring those observed in the female brain, which feels entitled and able to change Mr. Very Wrong into Mr. Right? Do they see themselves as the savior of American democracy? No one knows for sure, as everyone is differently-abled and operates out of their own motivations.

THE FAR LEFT OF THE SPECTRUM

Moving to the far left of the spectrum, launching the 70–80 percent of sapient-brained behavior populated by everyday survivors and thrivers, we leave the maladaptive landscape for those who are passionate—not about deception, lies, and cover-ups but about achievement by entering careers and endeavors as society's "movers and shakers." These individuals choose to live in social harmony even as they claim positions of power as CEOs, community leaders, and influential careers as passionate achievers.

The "salt of the earth," the largely anonymous survivors and thrivers whose courage can be observed in the lives of public figures such as kidnap victim Jaycee Lee Dugard, comprise the far left of the spectrum. For the entire expanse of this part of the spectrum, the term *psychopathy* is totally incorrect. Ironically, however, the same chemistry that ignites powerful brainmarks are displayed in those who survive and thrive and in those who become passionate achievers with a life-affirming gradational mix of nature via nurture—the ones most responsible for our continuation as a species. These are the passionate differently-abled individuals. Individuals such as Muhammad Ali, Elizabeth Arden, Truman Capote, Katharine Hepburn, Ted Turner, Mary Wollstonecraft Shelley, and Chesley "Sully" Sullenberger, who contribute positively to society, sometimes amassing wealth and influence and, in exemplary instances, becoming legitimate world changers through innovation, the latter personified in the likes of Steve Jobs, Ted Turner, and Bill Gates. Researchers such as Robert Hare (1993) and Martin Kantor (2006) present the notion that a spectrum of everyday psychopathy does indeed exist, but in differently-abled chemistry—not associated with arrogance or grandiose arrogance, but with hard work, tenacity, and resilience to make one's dreams come true.

Ancient survival scripts guide adaptation toward survival of the fittest, allowing us to be "tough as nails" due to nature's gift of powerful cascading chemistry, which is present at birth. History shows that, as a species, we have survived insults, plagues, and natural disasters in all millennial time-frames while remaining at the top of the food chain. We possess what might be called "special weapons and tactics" as vigorous brain conditions across the neurospectrum, enabling us to adapt on the fly and do whatever it takes to live another day.

As we rapidly transition from infancy to childhood and on into adolescence, our brain continually adapts from crawling to walking, to language acquisition and learning agendas, and to pair bonding through play and interaction with family, peers, and others. Even as seldom used neurons are being pruned away, helpful ones are retained and expanded. Puberty is the most important new challenge for young and developing brains due to the chemical tsunamis required for sexualizing our wondrous sapient brains—an absolute necessity for the creation of progeny and, hopefully, for choosing nurturing mates. We are so proficient at adaptation we scarcely notice how quickly and effectively we accomplish living in modern society. Soon, due to our gift of being differently-abled, we realize we can become as athletic and as academic as we want and accomplish almost anything we choose.

SPECTRUM LEARNERS: BOUTIQUE CLASSROOMS AND INNOVATIONS

So let's think out loud for a moment. If I may ask, as a 27-year veteran of the classroom, what's wrong with what has come to be called "boutique classrooms," especially in high school and college? Such a classroom would work this way: One day a week, "outside-the-box" thinking is the order of the day in all subjects. In such a session, creativity rather than mindlessly repetitive work or matter-of-fact lectures would be encouraged in individual and group assignments. Finding what works to make education exciting and relevant is the key to reversing many instances of "learning disorders." Considering old-school methods of instruction, it is a wonder that students have any creativity left in them by the time they graduate high school. New and innovative methods of delivering education are often the stimuli students need.

From our perspective, a vast majority of so-called learning disorders are, for the most part, not disorders at all but variations of adaptation producing *spectrum learners*. (Prescribing Ritalin to a six-year-old should be medical malpractice, in our humble opinion.) In a boutique classroom setting, a student who learns, reads, or computes math differently would simply adapt to his or her differently-abled brain's version of learning, arranging for longer study time and applying for slight changes in instruction such as tutorials and more time to take tests. This approach is becoming common practice, and it is the right thing to do in secondary and higher education for differently-abled brains. For every well-known innovator—Steve Jobs, Bill Gates, Albert Einstein—there are scores of anonymous over achievers.

Two personal examples of adaptation will illustrate my point. The first example involves my hearing. About five years ago, I realized it was not what it used to be. The popular way to handle hearing loss is to visit a hearing-aid clinic, where the diagnosis of hearing loss is followed rapidly by a sales pitch certain to include several models of expensive hearing aids. The less popular option—doing nothing—allows the hearing organs time to adapt to aging neurons. As we age, our hearing will diminish somewhat. Living tissue changes. I chose not to visit a clinic. Steadily, over the next few years, although my hearing diminished, it leveled off and actually improved. It may never be at the level I once enjoyed in youth and early middle age, but I am not wearing an expensive hearing aid. Now I simply tell students to "speak up when asking questions." I have convinced myself I hear just fine.

The second example involves a routine visit to the dentist. Some time ago I was informed that I had gum loss. "Do you want to keep your teeth?" I was asked. At this diagnosis, many in the dental chair panic and settle for expensive dental work. But gum loss is unavoidable as one ages. We may choose to rev up our brushing or purchase a food particle remover—you know, the ones that vibrate and gush water. We also can opt to brush and continue to floss as usual and expect to have improved dental health, albeit with somewhat diminished gums. As we age, we change and experience some loss due to aging tissue. We make an effort to get in better shape and improve nutritional choices and move on. We have losses, sagging, wrinkles, stooping, and some weight gain. We make adjustments and get over it, and we allow our sapient brains and bodies time to adapt to strategies such as increased exercise and better nutrition.

The point is this: Sapient brains are built to adapt, so when variations of adaptation occur, as observed in aging, individuals thus afflicted seek to adapt to the new imperatives. Similarly, an adolescent who weathers a "first love" breakup with a natural reaction of sadness may be unnecessarily sent to a therapist or, worse, given antidepressant medication instead of allowing the broken heart time to heal naturally. Given time, most affect (emotional) adaptations are corrected by those experiencing such conditions by calling upon their natural abilities of adaptation. The saying "Time heals all wounds," though extremely broad, holds some measure of wisdom in the ways of modern sapient brain functioning.

In the same vein, some previously diagnosed "disorders" have been edited out of the DSM, no longer to be considered clinical disorders by therapists. For example, homosexuality, once considered a disorder, was reversed as such in the heavily edited 1973 version of the DSM before complete removal in 1986. Frankly, psychology in general, and clinical psychology in particular, has experienced many misfires and miscalculations based upon diagnostic criteria that are little more than myths calculated to "recruit" clients. For further edification of the misdeeds of clinical psychology, please refer to the excellent book *Eleven Blunders that Cripple Psychotherapy in America* (Cummings and O'Donohue 2008).

If sapient brains possessed as many disorders as suggested by DSM diagnostic criteria, we would have become extinct millennia ago. How many times, for example, must neuroscience show proof that antisocial personality disorder is not in the same orbit as pathological psychopathy, or that psychopathy is not necessarily a disorder at all? In fact, as we contend, adaptive versions allow our species to survive and thrive to make another run at successful adaptations and create progeny. Adaptive versions are just the tip of the iceberg across the neurospectrum. Without powerful cascading chemistry and a fully functioning PFC, we would not be survivors, thrivers, achievers, or world-changing innovators. Take Kim Peek, the original "Rain Man," as a prime example of a differently-abled person.

MAKING THE CASE FOR THE DIFFERENTLY-ABLED I: KIM PEEK (1951–2009)

Kim Peek

| adaptive | passionate achiever | maladaptive |
| survivors | thrivers | corruptive | pathological |

All we need is love.

Kim Peek

A *savant* is defined as an eminent scholar with prodigious mental skills and knowledge. Scientists who studied Kim Peek's phenomenal skills across 15 categories referred to his genius as "mega-savant." For instance, Peek had memorized 12,000 books, including the entire Bible—yet he struggled with routine activities such as getting dressed and leaving his home. How could his brain be so differently-abled as to allow him to read one page of a book with his left eye and the other page with his right eye?

In 1984, writer Barry Morrow met Peek in Arlington, Texas. The meeting inspired Morrow to write the screenplay for what would become the hit movie *Rain Man,* starring Dustin Hoffman. The movie swept the major categories of the 1988 Academy Awards, as well as the Golden Globe awards, including Best Picture, Best Director, Best Screenplay, and Best Actor for Hoffman's riveting performance. Hoffman met Peek in preparation for his role, and after gaining some insight into Peek's remarkable abilities, he told Peek's father to "share him with the world" (*Weekly World News,* December 2, 2009). Later, Morrow gave Peek the Oscar he won for writing the best screenplay.

Slowly, Peek overcame some of his social insecurities, including his literal interpretation of life, which he combated by telling jokes. He spent the next 20 years amazing audiences with his phenomenal recall. His father stood beside him all the way and refused to institutionalize his son.

Neurologically, Peek was born with *macrocephaly,* damage to the cerebellum and a missing corpus callosum, a condition that did not allow the left hemisphere of his brain to communicate with the right hemisphere. He had difficulty with motor skills, not walking until age four, and he scored low on conventional intelligence tests. Later, when he was diagnosed as "retarded," doctors suggested he would do better in a permanent home for individuals with developmental disorders.

In 2004, the Center for Bioinformatics at the NASA Ames Research Center in California used CAT and MRI scans to study Peek's brain. In 2008, further study diagnosed Peek with FG syndrome, a rare disorder linked to the X chromosome, producing physical abnormalities such as macrocephaly (abnormally large head) and hypotonia (weak muscles). Following a heart attack, Peek died in 2009.

MAKING THE CASE FOR THE DIFFERENTLY-ABLED II: TRUMAN CAPOTE (1924–1984)

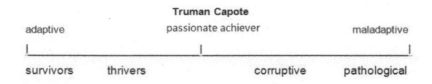

Failure is the condiment that gives success its flavor.

Truman Capote

Born Truman Streckfus Persons in New Orleans, Louisiana, American author Truman Capote, known for short stories, novels, plays, and novellas such as *Breakfast at Tiffany's* (1958), singlehandedly created the nonfiction true-crime novel with the publication in 1966 of *In Cold Blood.* Novelist and friend Harper Lee (*To Kill a Mockingbird,* 1960) traveled to Kansas with Capote as he examined the continuous yet oddly nurturing relationship between two ex-cons—psychopath Perry Edward Smith and perpetual loser Richard Hickok. Smith would be the gunman who murdered four members of the Clutter family in their Holcomb, Kansas, farmhouse. Capote spent the best part of six years researching and developing the story, which would create a new genre: the nonfiction true-crime novel. The retelling of this horrific crime remains Capote's most revered work.

Capote never recovered from his research and was unable to complete another project. *Capote* the 2005 movie depicting the research and writing of *In Cold Blood,* contains dialogue between Capote and Smith, the shooter, in which Capote admits the similarity of their troubled upbringing: "We both emerged from the darkness of our troubles. You [Smith] came out the backdoor. I came out the front door of our childhoods" (*Lawrence Journal World,* April 3, 2005). The main difference between the writer and the killer he wrote about? A differently-abled brain.

Chapter 4

The Psychopath Alarm and Why It Fails

READERS' PRE-TEST

The *psychopath alarm* is the

a. hypothalamus
b. hippocampus
c. medial forebrain bundle
d. amygdala
e. limbic system

The answer is *d,* the amygdala.

THE ART OF PAYING ATTENTION

The amygdala, an almond-shaped mass of neurons that sends alerts as "chills down our spine"—signals that make us feel "creepy" and unsettled—allows us to spot the red flags of deception from those "auditioning" in front of us. Yet there exists a formidable problem with this alarm. Initially, as we observe a handsome (or beautiful) face glowing with charm and charisma, we may not realize that surface appearances are often deceptive. What if the camera-friendly face oozing with charm is actually hiding arrogance and possibly dangerously psychopathic behavior? We wouldn't know until later, when it's too late. We must be aware that a Mr. Hyde may reside behind all the charm, and that he may be using that charm as a lure. Females in particular are fooled by charm: By nature and as a neurotruth, the female brain is vulnerable to a handsome and charming male (or female).

Sadly, psychopaths are adept at fooling Mother Nature. Nature's gift—the amygdala—nestled within our medial temporal lobes, is constructed to warn us of danger from strangers and others who pose threats to our physical well-being. Yet a handsome (or beautiful face) filled with charm and charisma appears engaging and thus not threatening, so it is possible for not a single behavioral signal—sight, sound, or smell—of "creepiness" or imminent danger to emanate from the person "auditioning" in front of us. In pathological psychopathy, it's only later the "foul and awful" predator arises, and by then it's too late—the trapdoor spider has emerged.

We embrace *evolutionary neuropsychology* (how our vigorous brain conditions develop, adapt, and at times maladapt over millennia) as the best choice to merge with *behavioral neuroscience*—our preferred paradigms in all things pertaining to vigorous brain conditions, including psychopathy. This chapter addresses important survival questions in our struggle for existence. First, can the amygdala ignore charm and charisma and look beneath the surface for mixed signals? As all of us who study the scientific aspects of psychopathy know, the answer is maybe; that is, when one pays attention to red flags as there is nothing in the surface behavior or demeanor of a psychopath that can be detected. There is nothing in the surface behavior or demeanor of a psychopath that can be detected. More troubling is a second question: Are psychopaths too deceptive for the alarm? Thankfully, and as we will see, the answer is no.

The person standing before us (usually a male) who is auditioning (for a female) projects all of his gushing charm, charisma, and smooth-talking "gift of gab" as candy to the female brain; she finds him engaging and sexy. This may, however, be the first red flag that a cruelly self-absorbed and entitled psychopath lies beneath a highly deceptive persona. Although nature cannot help us with this first red flag, if the person standing before us appears too good to be true, he probably is. His deception reinforces our first red flag—he has a lot to hide. In other words, the handsome, charming male may be hiding his real side—the Hyde side—and that, in fact, is our first red flag. But our amygdala missed it because of his deception. In essence, the psychopath fooled Mother Nature.

This chapter also addresses our central concern that it's high time to acknowledge our brain—and our brain alone—as the centerpiece of human experiences, along with our accompanying gifts of nature: powerful cascading chemistry, neuroglia, and the hormones of our endocrine glands. All told, these neurological regions provide the drive chain of the idiosyncratic "special weapons and tactics" in our cortical tissue, which interprets and detects experiences producing our unique perceptions. Author Anaïs Nin had it right when she said, "We don't see the world as it is. We see it as we are." We take it Nin was speaking about our differently-abled abilities of perception most geared to adaptation, but in those with differently-abled brains, adaptation transitions into maladaptation, producing instances of criminality and varieties of corruptive psychopathy.

At the same time, it is important for readers to know that modern neuropsychology and evolutionary psychology reject the clinical, psychiatric, or medical model perspectives as problematic in interpreting our shared human condition. It is *res ipsa* evident that such traditional perspectives add unnecessary layers of analyses focused on personality disorders requiring differential diagnoses from a manual—the DSM—that has quadrupled in size since 1952. Outwardly, clinicians and psychiatrists subscribe to this profit-driven manual as an expanded "clinical tool," while inwardly they celebrate more ways to exact profits from the sale of psychoactive drugs. It is common knowledge that rampant abuses have already been uncovered as "terrible mistakes" (misdiagnoses) due to the DSM. As author and journalist Jon Ronson (2011, 35) states, "Maybe the American Psychiatric Association had a crazy desire to label all life a mental disorder." And this from DSM-V (the fifth edition, 2013) editor Dr. Allen Frances: "[DSM collaborators] have made some terrible mistakes. . . . It's very easy to set off a false epidemic in psychiatry. . . . We inadvertently contributed to three that are ongoing now: autism, attention deficit, and childhood bipolar, . . . and [speaking of the autism mistake] . . . many kids who would have been eccentric, different, were suddenly labeled autistic (Ronson 2011, 234–235). It is easy to see why progression in understanding the roots and continual adaptation of our human condition must always embrace evolutionary neuropsychology and behavioral neuroscience.

As author Patricia Cornwell states in *Portrait of a Killer* (2002, 62), "Recycled inaccuracies that have metastasized from one book to another [must be avoided]." If I may, recycled inaccuracies are all you get when following traditions from the so-called medical model or clinical psychology. It's not that all clinical psychologists and psychiatrists are misinformed and/or greedy, but it's close to that. It's similar to saying "all football players retire with some brain damage," as many of them do, and in about the same percentages of psychopathy and maladaptation (about 20–30 percent), with serious symptoms catching up to them when they are 40 to 45 years of age.

Prior to just a few years ago, psychopathy had long been defined as an accumulation of disorders, usually of "personality"—whatever that is—or of moral character deficits, or as an antisocial personality disorder. So strictly speaking, over the expanse of three decades, psychopathy became, most notably, antisocial personality disorder (APD), sometimes with tangential characteristics of narcissistic personality disorder (NPD) as reflected in the pages of the DSM-IV-TR. Misfires and blunders in this definition? Yes, absolutely. Misfires and blunders have been consistent and glaring in clinical psychology for decades (see Cummings and O'Donohue 2008).

ACTUAL, FACTUAL NEUROTRUTHS

Neurotruth 1: As FBI investigators John Douglas and Robert Ressler discovered, psychopaths by their own admission never "suffer," something that is required in diagnosing personality disorders in the DSM. The most widely respected psychopathy researcher in the world, Robert D. Hare, is the first to agree: "To elaborate, psychopaths are generally well satisfied with themselves and with their inner landscape. . . . They see nothing wrong with themselves. . . . They experience little personal distress, and find their behavior rational, rewarding, and satisfying" (Hare 1993, 195).

Neurotruth 2: "Cognitive therapy" actually makes psychopaths worse. There is little scientific evidence that psychopaths respond favorably to *any* treatment or intervention (Raine and Sanmartin 2001; Hare 1993). When will clinicians and psychiatrists come to their collective senses and recognize that psychopaths feel empowered, entitled, and sexual in the continuation of their deceptive practices?

THE PARALIMBIC SYSTEM

Within sapient brains, a region known as the *paralimbic system* appears as an innermost ring within the deepest cortical recesses of sapient brains. This region alone is responsible for defining some of our most treasured human emotional and cognitive experiences; it is the region most responsible for our abilities to live and work in social harmony. It provides brain-marks by assigning emotional values to experiences, allowing decision making to mitigate impulsivity as well as high-order thinking and reasoning in solving everyday problems. Collectively, does this region hold ancient secrets in the emergence of psychopathic traits? Judging by the evidence that follows, the answer is overwhelmingly yes.

Neuroscans (high-resolution brain scans) reveal seven regions within this neurological system that can become underdeveloped, traumatized, or somehow rendered maladaptive:

- The *anterior cingulate*—the site for decision making, empathy, and affect—when maladapted dampens such strikingly human conditions as empathy and affect. Thus emotions that are blunted or inappropriately expressed are characteristics of psychopathy.

- The *orbitofrontal prefrontal cortex* (OPFC) produces rational decision making, thus controlling impulsivity and allowing for behavioral flexibility and cognitive reconsideration—the "second thoughts" of an adult brain—yet in maladaptation, impulsivity and the inability to learn from mistakes arises, thus replacing the "steady hand" of cognitive reconsideration.
- The *ventromedial prefrontal cortex* merges feelings with cognitive "brainstorming" so cognitive decisions are arrived through the filter of emotion; in maladaptation, emotions appear diminished or inappropriate (as when laughter is expressed when sadness would have been appropriate).
- In posterior regions of the paralimbic system, the *posterior cingulate* processes emotions connected to emotional memory for quick processing; in maladaptive examples, actions become disconnected from memory, as is often observed in horrific crimes.
- The *insula* alerts mind to pain perception, especially disgust; in maladaptation, high tolerance to pain and a failure to feel disgust are observed.
- The *temporal lobe* in adaptation integrates emotion, perception, and social interactional cues; in maladaptation, empathy disintegrates and becomes disconnected from social cues.
- The *amygdala* is the fear "alarm"; in a maladapted amygdala, the person acts fearlessly, as though danger never existed.

THE RISE OF NEUROTRUTH

So where does behavioral evidence for psychopathy come from? From vigorous brain conditions, not "personality disorders," as I have detailed in *Analyzing Criminal Minds* (Jacobs 2011). If we take the high road suggested by neuroscience and evolutionary neuropsychology's insistence upon presenting and understanding vigorous brain conditions as the source for psychopathy, we will find neurotruths (ibid.). Below are examples of neurotruths relative to psychopathy and rationale for why our natural psychopathy alarm may not work.

Take for example, *Neurotruth 12*: What the world continues to call "psychopathy" (incorrectly, as only the far right of neurospectrum correctly identifies corruptive and pathological psychopaths) is due to vigorous brain conditions from powerful endogenous chemistry, neuroglia, and hormones. These powerful chemicals, hormones, and neuroglia comprise the neurospectrum of both life-affirming and life-corrupting activities, the lion's share being 70–80 percent of the neurospectrum to the far left and midline, in contrast to only 20–30 percent of the neurospectrum to the right of midline and terminating at the far right (both varieties deserving the term *psychopathy*).

Vigorous brain conditions observed as psychopathic are driven by perversions of excitatory and inhibitory chemistry and are exacerbated by perverted neurocognitive mapping in extreme gradations. All told, these downsides are steep and thus produce variations of the arrogance required to define corruptive psychopathy and pathological (violent) psychopathy.

PSYCHO AND FEAR

In 1960, the black-and-white movie sensation *Psycho*, directed by Alfred Hitchcock from a novel by Robert Bloch (1959), portrays psychopath Norman Bates (played by Anthony Perkins) as a young man with limited social skills who nevertheless is engaging to women as a shy and lonely sad sack. Such behavior, usually deserving of sympathy, fools lodger Marion Crane (played by Janet Leigh). Soon after meeting Crane, Bates proves to be other than what he presents himself to be. Hiding his psychopathic dirty tricks in deceptive practices—including killing his own mother—he is, in fact, far more dangerous, more arrogant, than he appears. Clearly, Crane's psychopathy alarm is silenced, and she also, unknowingly, sexually arouses Norman, opening up yet another can of worms. She never sees the real Norman, even as he, wearing the dress and wig of his dead mother (ultimately his "protector"), attacks and murders her in the movie's unforgettable "shower scene."

Norman's sad-sack charm and boyish good looks circumnavigate Marion's brain, specifically, her amygdala; she responds only to the behavior Norman presents, thus showing her nurturing side, filled with sympathy for his lonely life. In *Psycho*, we can interpret *res ipsa* how a smart woman like Crane, who was entrusted by her boss to help manage financial matters, misses Norman's pathological psychopathy. The fact is, Bates does not present that brain to Crane. We must never forget the extent of deceptive practices, sexualized "dirty tricks," and animal "smarts" possible from corruptive and pathological psychopaths. To borrow an analogy from Robert Louis Stevenson's *Strange Case of Dr. Jekyll and Mr. Hyde* (1886), those who knew Henry Jekyll saw only Dr. Jekyll and never Mr. Hyde; when Hyde emerged, he did so rapidly and deadly, like a trapdoor spider—too late for the amygdala, even as it finally signaled danger.

NORMAN BATES AND DAVID MCCALL

Fast forward 38 years to David McCall (portrayed by Mark Wahlberg), the latest cinematic version of pathological psychopathy, in *Fear* (1986).

In this movie, Nicole Walker, McCall's target, goes much further than Marion Crane does in *Psycho* by expressing her love for David in feeling sexual and empowered by his touch. She experiences romantic and sexual intoxication in the guise of a handsome and charming male who oozes sexuality. Only the signal of this charmer—the person Nicole experiences—explains why her alarm fails too, even as it did for her mom, Laura (Amy Brenneman), and Nicole's friend Margo (Alyssa Milano). None of them see the real David. Yet the psychopathy alarm works to perfection for Nicole's father, Steven Walker (played by William Petersen), who tells his wife, "There's something wrong with him" and, finally, "David is a psychopath." Interestingly, the women—Marion, Nicole, Laura, and Margo—were all summarily blindsided by handsome, charming males—Norman and David—as they demonstrated charm and nonthreatening behavior in the audition process.

Are female brains vulnerable to being blindsided by handsome and charming males? To reiterate, the answer is yes, absolutely, and it explains why the amygdala fails. This is a foundational neurotruth of sapient brains.

MORE NEUROTRUTHS

Female sapient brains are vulnerable to the charms of handsome males who possess the gift of gab, who weave lies and half-truths around women in masterful deceptions. Consequently, the female feels sympathy for some and love for the special ones—the ones who stimulate her lust chemistry—such as the amphetamine-like PEA (phenylethylamine), which produces powerful romantic rushes as cascading chemistry, cemented later by her pair-bonding chemistry from industrial-strength oxytocin. This occurs in addition to powerful, pleasure-driven, and passionate chemistry from DANE (dopamine [DA] and norepinephrine [NE]) brain and other reward chemistry. It is easy to see from applied neuropsychology how a female's own chemistry overwhelms and convinces her. To sum it up, *females are vulnerable to the charms of handsome males.*

Across all relationships, females tend to pair bond too quickly and refuse to budge from their choice of Mr. Right. As strong evidence mounts indicating her choice is more aligned with Mr. Very Wrong, she relies on her female intuition (all is not lost), which she trusts explicitly, enhanced by DANE brainmarks, PEA brainmarks, and her quick-acting pair bonder, oxytocin. This solidifies her largely emotional choice—a choice sealed with her SANE brainmark (Serotonin), which guarantees she believes she *can* change him and *will* change him. Showing tenacity, hardheadedness, and willpower, she steadfastly clings to her choice of Mr. Right, even if he is Mr. Very Wrong in everyone else's eyes. Sadly, she may continue to hold this "truth" as self-evident even as CPS takes her children.

JE NE SAIS QUOI

From antiquity, larcenists have stolen what is not theirs and celebrated their "smarts," empowerment, and entitlement to fooling others. In modern times, conniving wealth managers engineer massive Ponzi schemes and steal investors' fortunes, and corrupt politicians cozy up to big corporations, ready to engage in deceptive practices.

We are all vaguely aware of what the French call *je ne sais quoi,* which literally means "I don't know what" and describes someone's inexplicable charm and sex appeal. Powerful behavioral characteristics that motivate one to achieve are not per se perceived to be psychopathic. Rather, varieties of narcissism and entitlement in sapient brains are completely normal (as observed in teenagers) and can often lead to passionate ambition resulting in lofty accomplishments, innovation, and wealth accumulation, all while following the rules of society and living life in social harmony. Individuals who possess adaptive versions of what the world persists in calling psychopathy are still best described by another take on the French expression *je ne sais quoi:* "You have something I can't quite put into words."

Professor Robert Hare, who developed the PCL-R, has researched and written two excellent books that admit to a "psychopathy of everyday life" as well as more obvious criminal varieties: *Without Conscience* (1993) and, more recently (with Paul Babiak), *Snakes in Suits* (2006). Psychiatrist Martin Kantor has chimed in with his courageous book on the same theme, *The Psychopathy of Everyday Life* (2006).

Hare refers to criminal varieties as "interspecies predators" who commit cold-blooded rape and murder without empathy and conscience. In *Analyzing Criminal Minds* (Jacobs 2011) and *The Psychology of Deception* (2008b), I teased apart Hare's commonly used list that defines psychopathic traits into the characteristics, again *res ipsa* evident, in defining elements of telltale arrogance—perversion from grandiose narcissism that would otherwise be described as completely normal and practically guaranteeing success. In our view, the traits that contribute most to the maladaptation observed in arrogance are the following:

- A grandiose sense of self-worth
- Pathological lying
- Lack of remorse or guilt
- Lack of empathy
- Parasitic lifestyle

- Shallow affect (no emotional depth)
- Failure to accept responsibility for behavior
- Poor behavioral controls
- Criminal versatility (the most robust characteristics in corruptive and pathological varieties producing grandiose arrogance and a score of 30+ on the PCL-R)

The remaining characteristics are *res ipsa* evidence of traits observed in the 70–80 percent of the neurospectrum who do not deserve the label of *psychopathy*. They are the survivors and thrivers—what I refer to as "connivers," those who get what they want through manipulation of circumstances. They possess some of the following characteristics:

- A glib and superficial charm
- Cunning and manipulation
- A need for stimulation
- A proneness to boredom
- Promiscuous sexual behavior
- A lack of realistic long-term goals
- Impulsivity
- Irresponsibility
- Early behavioral problems
- Delinquent behavior as a juvenile
- Revocation of conditional release
- Many short-term marital relationships

For prey, the psychopathy alarm fails in signaling fear and exposing Mr. Hyde due to deceptions by calculating predators; they know exactly what they're doing and what it will take to be successful. Therefore, their targeted prey are blindsided by what appears to be at the most "the man of their dreams" or at the least "a nice guy who wouldn't hurt a flea." Yet later in the relationship, what amounts to a dangerous trapdoor spider may emerge.

What about the amygdala in predators? The tissue is nestled in their own brains and becomes maladapted—either it never developed normally or it was traumatized by some injury or from toxic parenting. Adaptation became maladaptive, producing the "mark" of psychopathy expressed by arrogance. Therefore, predators are afraid of nothing and stop at nothing to experience whatever they can imagine and whatever they desire—all "bundled" with no conscience, guilt, remorse, or empathy.

FINAL THOUGHTS

Why would someone so bloated with empowerment, entitlement, and arrogance ever imagine how life could be any better? How could Superman's cape of arrogance ever be improved upon? Why would they ever want to change? Arrogance creates the ultimate stranglehold on equality and noble achievements in life; never again will those thus differently-abled live in social harmony. The only role those who are maladapted in this way can imagine for themselves is predator—a panther to thin human herds.

I'll end this section with a quote from Professor Robert Hare: "With corporate psychopathy, it's a mistake to look at them as neurologically impaired. . . . It's easier to look at them from a Darwinian slant. It makes perfect sense from the evolutionary perspective. . . . They've got to misrepresent their resources . . . they've got to manipulate and con and deceive and be ready to move on as soon as things get hot" (Ronson 2011, 164).

MAKING THE CASE FOR THE DIFFERENTLY-ABLED I: BILL CLINTON (1946–)

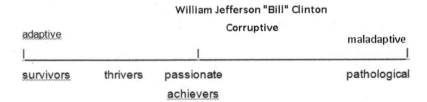

Listen to me, I'm going to say this again. I did not have sexual relations with that woman, Miss Lewinsky.

President Bill Clinton, January 26, 1998

I did have a relationship with Miss Lewinsky that was not appropriate. In fact, it was wrong.

President Bill Clinton, August 17, 1998

Seven months after admitting that he had lied about having a sexual relationship with White House intern Monica Lewinsky, Bill Clinton said he had not been candid for reasons of protecting his family from embarrassment. He said the relationship "constituted a critical lapse in judgment and a personal failure on my part for which I am solely and completely responsible" (*WashingtonPost.com,* August 18, 1998).

One would be hard pressed to find greater numbers of the moderately-abled varieties of grandiose ambition (mixed with tenacity and resilience) that often turns corruptive than with those who are in presidential politics. Take President William Jefferson "Bill" Clinton, the 42nd president of the United States (1993–2001) as our differently-abled example. For all of his educational preparation, innovative programs, and monumental accomplishments while in office, he will be forever remembered as a scandalous political survivor.

The former Yale Law School graduate (1973) returned to Arkansas in the mid-1970s, was elected governor in 1978, and was reelected in 1982. Ten years later, he defeated George H. W. Bush for president of the United States and was reelected in 1996. Two years into his second term, his real troubles began.

President Clinton was impeached by the U.S. House of Representatives on charges of perjury and obstruction of justice in December 1998—clearly corruptive actions if not for presidential politics. The Monica Lewinsky scandal and the Paula Jones lawsuit were the fuses for impeachment articles. Subsequently, Clinton was acquitted by the Democrat-controlled Senate; not surprisingly, partisan politics saved the job of "Slick Willie," as he became known in the media, but not his reputation, which will forever be tinged with scandal. It appears the political bad boy would have had it no other way. You "have to give people something to look forward to when they get up in the morning," he said in 2012 (*Amsterdam News,* February 15).

MAKING THE CASE FOR THE DIFFERENTLY-ABLED II: RICHARD NIXON (1913–1994)

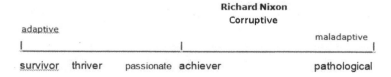

Power tends to corrupt, and absolute power corrupts absolutely.

Lord Acton

A man is not finished when he is defeated. He is finished when he quits.

Richard Nixon

Richard Milhous Nixon, the only politician to resign the office of president of the United States, served as a representative (1946) and later a senator (1950) from the state of California. He was a two-term vice president of the United States during the Eisenhower administration (1953–1961) and narrowly lost the presidency to John F. Kennedy in 1960. He lost the election for governor of California in 1962 but rebounded with resolve to win the presidency in 1968. He was reelected by a landslide in 1972.

The escalating Watergate scandal in Nixon's second term wrecked political support for him, forcing "Tricky Dick," the 37th president of the United States, to resign in August 1974 in the face of certain removal from office. In political history, the term *dirty tricks* as well as the word *plumbers* (in its political sense) entered the language forever in the aftermath of the break-in at the national Democratic Party's headquarters inside the Watergate Hotel in Washington, D.C., in 1972. It became clear in three articles of impeachment that President Nixon had attempted to use the CIA to halt the FBI investigation of possible criminal behavior and that he had abused the power of the presidency. Was Nixon's Committee to Re-elect the President (CREEP) responsible for a plethora of dirty tricks? Were illegal funds used to pay for the crimes and misdemeanors of those closest to the president? Did a sitting president cover up his knowledge of dirty tricks? Through it all, Nixon persisted with his own explanation of his actions: "I am not a crook."

Ultimately, mounting evidence confirmed that corruption and illegality had, in fact, been perpetrated, as well as covered up, sending Nixon, yet another instance in a long line of political corruptors holding the nation's highest office, into resignation.

PART II

The Story Behind the Story

Chapter 5

Passionate Brainmarks

READERS' PRE-TEST

From known cerebral regions producing powerful, front-loaded excitatory chemistry in youth, which of the following neurochemicals is usually considered the one most likely to trigger gratuitous violence when toxic or perverted?

a. DANE

b. PEA

c. dehydroepiandrosterone (DHEA)

d. testosterone

e. all of the above

The answer is *d,* testosterone.

Normal, extraordinary, abnormal, perverted, and violent sexuality—essentially all things sexual—is possible due to the powerful influence of dopamine and norepinephrine, or what we call DANE brain. Overcoming the modularly of serotonin (SA) and norepinephrine, or SANE brain, effects by DANE brain excitation, orgasms—the fireworks stand of vigorous brain conditions—are produced. There exists no other neurochemical protocol in the human mammalian nervous system comparable with DANE brain's sexual, erotic, lustful, and euphoric chemistry.

Sapient-brained species become sexual long before showing signs of being rational or reasonable. What's up with that? A high probability of creating progeny is the evolutionary answer, and that's precisely why we're all still around bathed in human drama.

(Jacobs 2013)

HEADQUARTERS FOR THINGS THAT GO BUMP IN THE NIGHT

Professor Jacobs's forensic psychology lab manual *Brainmarks* (2009) presents an adaptation versus maladaptation model of vigorous brain conditions based upon evolutionary psychology. Brainmarks represent brain conditions that produce, and are the result of, powerful neurochemistry and the hormones required for thinking, emotion and mood, and, ultimately, behavior. This model reinforces the evolutionary position of nature's gift of tenacity and resilience as the "roots" of definitive behavior in moderate regions of the neurospectrum.

To be clear, brainmarks is not a medical model sympathizer, meaning we are not focusing on disease and prescriptive medication as the way to health, nor do we side with psychiatry or clinical psychology—the disciplines that train "mental health specialists" in finding disorder and dysfunction. Rather, we make a book-length argument that we come into this world with nature's gift of tenacity in the struggle for existence. Vigorous brain conditions are the substance of our evolutionarily charged perspective, not "personality disorders"—whatever that is—requiring psychiatric or clinical diagnoses from a book characterized by dysfunction, disorders, and diseases appropriately called the *Diagnostic and Statistical Manual of Mental Disorders,* now in its fifth edition. From under 200 pages as a pamphlet in 1952, the latest edition is over 1,000 pages long. Here's a sure bet: If you visit a psychiatrist or psychologist, you will emerge from that visit with a diagnosis.

Let's define our powerful neurochemistry. Dopamine is a catecholamine, acting as an emotional "jazzer" and "energizer" of general as well as gender-specific behaviors. Like DA, norepinephrine in liberation produces laser-focused, goal-directed behavior. Cascading NE in the brain stimulates adrenaline in the body, which lies behind the well-documented fight-or-flight response. Chemical cascades of DA and NE (together in our reference to DANE brain) defines the rise of passionate, pleasurable, and sexual behavior. DANE brain is lust personified.

When coupled with maturation of the prefrontal cortex and well-crafted preparation and planning, behavior becomes turbocharged toward high achievement. In the female brain, DANE brain lies behind rewards from pleasurable activities such as sex (love), eating, dancing, and other activities linked to reward chemistry. For males—for instance, one dancing on a barroom table while stripped naked to the waist with a bra draped over his head—pleasure enhanced by intoxication creates a DANE brain moment. Guys play sports, race fast cars, and party with the girls while engaging DANE brains. No better motivators exist in gender differentiation, driven by DANE brainmarks, than varieties of anticipated pleasure from chemical fireworks igniting passion, foreplay, flirting in the anticipation of sex, winning some challenge, or being selected as a "hot body" by another "hot body" at bars and health clubs—modern society's watering holes.

In orgasm, DA increases sexual ecstasy in both male and female brains. Surging dopamine lies behind addictions, which originate in the "pleasure pathways" of the *midbrain limbic system* (MLS), reinforced by the *mesolimbic dopamine delivery system*—the *medial forebrain bundle* (MFB), the *ventral tegmental area* (VTA), and the *nucleus accumbens* (NAcc)—and resulting in dopamine spikes in areas of the brainstem and MLS and extending forward into the prefrontal cortex via *mesocortical dopamine pathways.* It is easy to see how entire brains can be highjacked by pleasure and lust spikes from reward centers across the expanse of cortical tissue. If DANE brain is not enough to jazz us sexually, the experience is turbocharged by testosterone and phenylethylamine in both genders.

DANE brain, PEA brain, and testosterone drive the propagation of the species from ancient scripts. Nothing gets us together faster than behavior driven by lust. The male version of DANE brain recognizes females' numerous "hormone markers" (flawless skin, glorious hair, sparkling eyes, lips and facial features, breasts, waist, hips, and legs), which transform him into a predatory forager, a person who must be addressed for what he is: a male out for sex. In the meantime, the female's DANE brain erupts when Prince Charming enters her life. If her cocktail of circulating chemistry is not enough, there's yet another aphrodisiac forthcoming in phenylethylamine, which produces the well-documented "romantic rush."

The PEA brainmark provides powerful amphetamine-like stimulation to visual and tactile aspects of gender-specific behavior. From her hormone markers characterizing feminine wiles to his masculine qualities signaling a low-fat, lightly muscled torso announcing strength and dominance, constant reminders of his and her brands of sexuality are focused by DANE brain, while the PEA brain provides romantic rushes for flirtatious histrionics and seductive glances.

For males and females pursuing their respective fantasies, adolescence is the developmental stage most impacted by DANE-PEA-testosterone cascades of the sort that produce parenting nightmares. When the female PEA brainmark peaks, she is focused like a laser, predictably on a handsome and charming male. Similarly, the same liberated brainmark in males produces *gawking behavior.* He can't keep his eyes off her. In contrast, she merely glances at him and can't help but smile. Lust does wonders in the sexualization of our species.

Students who have what I call quid pro quo PEA-brains always find ways to sit close to one another in class and to ostensibly "talk about class," leading to coffee, lunch, and who knows what else. In Asian philosophy, females are yin to males' yang, demonstrating the attraction between seemingly contrasting dynamics of physicality. There exists no feeling quite like the DANE-PEA-testosterone cascades so prevalent in adolescence. No wonder teenagers are sexually guided missiles with regard to each other during this very dangerous (but exciting) developmental stage.

ESTROGEN BRAINMARK

Estrogen is the ubiquitous hormone central to the understanding of the look and feel of female bodies as well as the feminization of female brains deep down in cortices, "marking" psychological dispositions and predispositions for nurturing and communication. In liberation (or high gain), estrogen stimulates female brain centers, resulting in empowering qualities of femininity; she feels powerful, esteemed, assertive, seductive, and sexual. In addition to brightened mood and affect, resilience in handing everyday problems is increased with cascading estrogen. With the estrogen brainmark in liberation, alpha females are forces of nature. Who can say no to her charms, beauty, grace, assertiveness, tenacity, and daring?

Males have their own supply of estrogen, which increases the male desire to cuddle, often observed as taking a snooze following dopamine spikes at orgasm and, to some extent, refining and sharpening relational skills with a chosen mate. Later in life, as testosterone weakens in gradational strength, the estrogen brainmark becomes more influential in the male physiology and brain. This effect increases by the sixth decade, when older fathers become fierce protectors of teenage children, and it also contributes to the later attentiveness of grandfathers.

TESTOSTERONE AND ANDROSTENEDIONE

As a gender-specific excitatory "jazzer" of behavior, testosterone lies beneath the brain's perception of lust and sex. In males, testosterone is the major androgen (male hormone) engineering masculine body design and brain wiring. In contrast to males' body design, no chemical changes are required to produce the female brain-body. At eight weeks gestation, the chemical action of the Y chromosome in the XY configuration of male fetuses provides the all-encompassing, yet less than 1 percent, difference of the male brain due to monumental testosterone cascades. This chemical event accounts for male sapient brains being differently-abled from female sapient brains. By this chemical process, communication centers in males' temporal lobes are reduced, while limbic centers, highlighting sexuality, aggression, and predatory behaviors, are expanded and enhanced. With testosterone liberation at puberty, combined with an active DANE brain, males feels bulletproof, aggressive, focused, and entitled in all things sexual. He aggressively pursues whatever he chooses, boosting his feelings of power. Liberated testosterone from his male brain wiring transforms his masculine physicality, enhancing seductive charms that transform him into a conniving sexual pursuit artist, able in a single bound to blindside most females, who by nature are vulnerable to his gender-specific charms.

Androstenedione is testosterone selected for secretion in the ovaries. A jazzer of sexuality and erotic thoughts observed in the essence of youthful experimentation, its cascades exude sexual adventure mandated by evolutionary designs. It decreases in menopause and disappears in lifeless ovaries. In males, this same hormone it is known as the "smell of manhood," bolstering sexual drive when poured into his sweat glands, especially during sex. Released from his torso as a *pheromone,* it makes the male appear more sexy and desirable to females, accentuated selectively by her PEA brain in romantic cascades.

DHEA: THE FOUNTAIN OF YOUTH

The steroid hormone DHEA, or dehydroepiandrosterone, naturally produced by the adrenal glands, is a chemical jazzer driving youthful exuberance—a chemical inoculation for energizing affect and mood, florid in male and female adolescence and extending into young adulthood. DHEA becomes scarce in middle to old age.

In its own way, male and female gender-specific, excitatory chemistry, via vigorous brain conditions, brings the sexes together for fun, profit, and the ancient obsession of producing progeny. To this point, we have discussed six excitatory chemicals that provide the "power and light" of foraging, interacting, experiencing sex and love, and striving to find passion in life for both genders. By name they are DA, NE, PEA, testosterone, estrogen, and DHEA.

OXYTOCIN

Oxytocin (or the OXY brainmark) circulates as the chemical "glue" of social and pair bonding, forging attachments from connection, intimacy, and the nurturing of friends, lovers, mates, and children. Similar to but stronger in gradational strength than the male *vasopressin,* oxytocin lies behind the natural female tendencies to be cuddly and nurturing, which are critical to connectivity in intimacy bonding.

When the female mind, set on sex, is being triple-teamed by DANE-PEA-testosterone (in what I refer to as the *jazzing chemistry of certain intimacy*), it is highly likely that sex is going to happen. Who's going to stop her? Her body language becomes the foreplay that informs males of her DANE brain plans.

The male version of the OXY brainmark increases empathy and exists for the foundation of building trust, romanticism (males are often far more romantic than once thought), and social bonding. He becomes capable of "being Dad" and nurturing his own children. Stress hormones and blood pressure are reduced and replaced with "secure feelings." To a male brain in the grip of oxytocin, there's no place like home.

PROGESTERONE

Progesterone is an important modulator to estrogen and a precursor to *allopregnenolone,* the female brain's calming chemistry. In scarcity, low-gain progesterone acts as a reversal of estrogen's mood brighteners, producing *premenstrual syndrome* (PMS) and its emotional script of irritability. In female and male brains, progesterone supports the normal development of neurons (brain cells) and exerts a protective and ameliorative effect on damaged cerebral tissue.

Likewise, the male version of progesterone is required for the production of testosterone from his testes, helping balance his estrogen levels. Progesterone and testosterone contribute to strong bone development in males.

CORTISOL, VASOPRESSIN, AND PROLACTIN

Cortisol, a stress hormone, is the chemical antithesis of estrogen in its production of a thick mane of lustrous hair, soft and smooth skin, and an array of striking female hormone markers. In high gain, cortisol articulates into "stressed-out" behavior. A female looks stressed and often has frizzled hair and a frazzled physical appearance; in males, cortisol escalates behavior into angry outbursts and perhaps drives aggression into physical altercations such as "road rage" and physical assaults.

Vasopressin plays a key role in homeostasis by regulating water, glucose, and salts in the blood. Most of the chemical is stored in the endocrine system's posterior pituitary gland for release into the bloodstream. It plays an important role in pair bonding, social behavior, and maternal responses to stress. Besides its role in prosocial bonding, vasopressin can act as an attack molecule, characterized by territoriality and male-on-male aggression. Vasopressin in females lies beneath the subtle male characteristics of sexual assertiveness.

In females, *prolactin* stimulates lactation (the secretion of milk production). In males, it transforms the normally predatory male brain into "Mr. Mom," fostering paternal behavior and decreasing the drive for sexual conquests.

MULLERIAN INHIBITING SUBSTANCE (MIS)

Prior to the Y chromosome–mandated testosterone wash at eight weeks, the developing fetus can go either way, developing a brain that is wired either male or female. This is possibly due to the presence of both Wolffian ducts (micro-ducts capable of producing male genitals and internal male "plumbing") and Mullerian ducts (micro-ducts capable of producing female genitals and internal female sex organs). Both ducts are present side by side and ready to be fired up with stimulating and regulating chemistry.

Mullerian inhibiting substance (MIS) is a hormone produced by the Sertoli cells of fetal testes (following the testosterone wash) that stimulates regression and destruction of the Mullerian ducts, thus effectively ending hopes for birthing a baby girl. By the action of MIS, all evidence of what could have been female (physical reproductive organs and feminine gender-specific orientation) is terminated in favor of a male gender-specific body, accompanied by a masculinized brain due to copious amounts of testosterone.

THE CHEMISTRY DRIVING NATURAL SELECTION

Truly, what a difference less than 1 percent of genetic priming makes in male versus female brains. As we noted earlier, it takes a transforming cascade of testosterone in the womb to change the default setting of female to male. Brains are wired male and external genitalia accompanied by internal "plumbing" develop due to the action of the Y chromosome, which triggers the testosterone wash. By this biologically mandated process, Wolffian ducts are activated while Mullerian ducts are absorbed by the body. We can say with certainty that "female" is the default setting for sapient brains. This brain condition is not in the least surprising when considering evolutionary designs, with priority given to females as possessors of the evolutionary treasure of ova (eggs) and a brain crafted by nature to be nurturing. "A machine (a female brain) like that is built for *connection*," notes. "That's the main job of the girl brain, and that's what drives a female to do from birth. This is the result of millennia of genetic and evolutionary hardwiring that once had—and probably still has—real consequences for survival" (Brizendine 2010, 20).

Due to cascading hormones, female behavior is often described, perhaps stereotypically, by the need to make emotional connection to others, a proficiency in verbal communication, and an ability to read body language. All three attributes turn out to be absolutely true and indicative of her brain condition in the presence of liberated (cascading) estrogen. She connects to friends, colleagues, and lovers with communication and with a heightened emotional memory for events. This condition baffles male brains not hardwired to these conditions—brain conditions nonetheless required in socialization in families, for raising children, and for cooperation in communities.

Male and female brains arrive at birth "factory sealed," prewired with important gender differences. Such sapient behavior as emotional sensitivity, connection to others, and verbal virtuosity are clearly female gender specifics. It has been estimated males use about 7,000 words a day in contrast to females, who use roughly three times as many, and that females speak of a rate of approximately 250 words per minute, versus the 125 per minute rate for males (Brizendine 2010, 14).

MAKING THE CASE FOR THE DIFFERENTLY-ABLED I: HELEN GURLEY BROWN (1922–2012)

Helen Gurley Brown

adaptive   passionate achiever   maladaptive

I_____I_____I

survivors   thrivers   corruptive   pathological

Helen Gurley grew up in near poverty-stricken conditions in Arkansas. She lost her father to an elevator accident when she was just 10 years old, and five years later, her sister Mary contracted polio, adding more emotional baggage to the skinny teenager's life. Upon relocating with her mother and sister to Los Angeles, Helen graduated from Woodbury Business College (1947). After working for the William Morris Agency and two other similar firms, she was hired by the Foote, Cone, and Belding advertising agency as a secretary. Noticing her writing skills, the wife of her boss suggested she be given the chance to write advertising copy, a position in which she excelled. Eventually she made her mark as one of the highest paid advertising copywriters in the country (*Encyclopedia Britannica,* 15th ed., s.v. "Helen Gurley Brown").

Helen's mother was quick to give good advice: She suggested Helen, who as a young teen was flat-chested and thin, her face marked by acne scars, excel in being smart instead of trying to be beautiful. Still, Helen entered one beauty contest after the other, failing to win each time. Nevertheless, she finally won a contest that guaranteed a trip to Hawaii. On this trip she landed another copywriting job and was given the Catalina swimsuit account.

Helen, enjoying dating and making nightly forays into Los Angeles night life, soon saved enough money to pay cash for a Mercedes-Benz automobile. This purchase became fortuitous as Helen was noticed in her new car by film producer David Brown, who was impressed that this young woman drove such as status symbol. As he had already been married (and was older), he informed her he would like to continue their relationship but preferred not to marry. She waived her hand in his face, said good-bye, and left. It took Brown two weeks to find her. After a few more delays, they finally married in 1959.

Helen had won the matrimonial sweepstakes. David Brown and Helen Gurley became a power couple, and their financial reward was beyond anyone's expectations. A movie producer, David Brown would eventually produce (along with Richard Zanuck) highly successful movies such as

The Sting (1973), *Jaws* (1973), *Cocoon* (1985), *Driving Miss Daisy* (1989), and *A Few Good Men* (1992), among others.

Helen was about to be launched into the stratosphere as well. Between jobs, she looked around for her next venture. David convinced her to write a book about her single life, and at age 40, Helen published *Sex and the Single Girl* (1962), which became an instant hit. She would write eight more books, but it was her first book that led to the biggest gamble of her life. She was given a one-year contract to take over a conservative magazine that was about to go into bankruptcy. The magazine was *Cosmopolitan,* and the rest of the story is history as one of the most famous turnarounds in magazine publishing. *Cosmopolitan* became, practically overnight, the most read young women's magazine in the country and Helen's private pulpit for sharing her thoughts and advice with readers. She countered *Playboy* magazine founder Hugh Hefner's famous centerfolds with several of her own male centerfolds, featuring the likes of Burt Reynolds, former football player Jim Brown, and TV personality John Davidson. The UK version of *Cosmo* continued this tradition into modern times.

During the 1960s, Helen was an outspoken advocate of women's sexual liberation, claiming women could have it all—love, sex, and money, a proposition that collided with traditional views of marriage and family. Yet it struck a chord with young women, and copies of *Cosmopolitan* continued to fly off magazine shelves, especially on college campuses. For decades to come, Helen, through *Cosmo,* led the charge of women's liberation—before the likes of feminists Betty Freidan, Germaine Greer, and Gloria Steinem, the latter the editor-in-chief of *Ms.* magazine.

The editor-in-chief behind *Cosmo* advocated that women be glamorous fashion mavens who used their smarts and well as their beauty to get what they wanted. Women who followed her advice came to be known as "*Cosmo* Girls." Helen Gurley Brown influenced three decades of women during her 32-year reign at *Cosmopolitan.* When she left the magazine, *Cosmo* was celebrating its 16th straight year as the number one best seller on college campuses and the number six best seller for general magazines. Helen lived a life of enormous influence due to passion, drive, her work ethic, and the ability to adapt across three decades of *Cosmopolitan* influence.

In 2008, Helen was named the 13th most powerful American over 80 years of age. David Brown died at age 93 on February 1, 2010, after 50 years of marriage to the woman who changed everything for other women. Helen and David established the David and Helen Gurley Brown Institute for Media Innovation, housed in the Columbia University Graduate School of Journalism and Stanford University Engineering School.

MAKING THE CASE FOR THE DIFFERENTLY-ABLED II: MARY WOLLSTONECRAFT SHELLEY (1797–1851)

Mary Shelley

adaptive   passionate achiever   maladaptive

|_____|_____|

survivors   thrivers   corruptive   pathological

Mary Shelley lived a literary life filled with what she called "a steady purpose," derived from her version of the human condition, which was characterized by survival, tenacity, resilience, hope, and love. Shortly after giving birth, Mary's mother, Mary Wollstonecraft, developed puerperal poisoning. She died 10 days later, leaving behind a daughter, also named Mary—Mary Wollstonecraft Godwin—who would grow into adolescence to have an affair at age 17 with a married man: Percy Shelley, 22 years of age. Later in life, Mary Shelley would survive the deaths of three of her four children; only her last child, Percy Florence, survived into adulthood.

Later, she would write the semiautobiographical *Mathilda,* a novella with the theme of father-daughter incestuous love. A few years later she almost died of a miscarriage. In the same year she lost Percy, her beloved husband, at sea (1822). She lived alone for almost 30 years before dying of a brain tumor in 1865 at the age of 53.

As an 18-year-old teenager, on the occasion of a writing contest, Mary Shelley wrote a short essay that would become an installment of one of the most celebrated Gothic novels of all time—*Frankenstein; or, The Modern Prometheus* (1818). The novel was published when Mary was 21. Frankenstein's monster has inspired over 50 films, including James Whale's version (1931) starring Boris Karloff and a comedic parody, *Young Frankenstein* (1974), directed by Mel Brooks and starring Gene Wilders as Dr. Frankenstein and Peter Boyle as the monster. Faithful to the book was director Kenneth Branagh's *Mary Shelley's Frankenstein* (1994).

Mary's literary achievements and her striking tenacity, resilience, and resolve powered her literary achievements and inoculated her against sadness, despair, loss of her children, and loss of her beloved husband. As a result, she was an achiever and a survivor par excellence who excelled as a Gothic novelist, dramatist, essayist, travel writer, and editor of the literary works of husband, Percy Bysshe Shelley.

Chapter 6

Modulating Brainmarks

READERS' PRE-TEST

What is the name of the neurotransmitter required to be liberated that becomes the most important for keeping people together when lust chemistry dries up?

a. norepinephrine
b. gamma-aminobutyric acid (GABA)
c. beta-endorphin
d. serotonin
e. PEA
f. DHEA

The answer is *d,* serotonin.

SEROTONIN AND THE SANE BRAIN

In this chapter, we address the function of inhibitory chemistry for gradations producing characteristics across the neurospectrum of both adaptive and maladaptive chemistry. It is our hypothesis that given insufficient serotonin efficacy, chemical conditions become ripe for arrogance, corruption, and a pathology deserving of the tag of psychopathy.

Might a rise in excitatory testosterone unchallenged by inhibitory and modulating chemistry from SANE brain and enhanced by PFC inhibitory control make conditions ripe for the self-indulgent corruption observed in former Illinois governor Rod Blagojevich and former investor Bernard Madoff? (See the epilogue.) This and other issues related to the chemical equation for psychopathy starts with a discussion of the soothing neurotransmitter serotonin 5-hydroxytryptamine, or more simply, 5-HT.

Following, we will illustrate the importance of the serotonin brainmark in creating and maintaining civilized society. Adults, with strong serotonin brains, glaringly absent for the most part in adolescents. With sane brains we find a spirit of cooperation, patience, and "second thoughts." A high-gain serotonin brain characterized by liberated 5-HT produces an engaging, nonthreatening, and quietly confident person, someone who displays better moods at work and at play and possesses self-control and a willingness to talk things over. This brainmark, along with a mature prefrontal cortex—the last component of the frontal lobes to fully develop in sapient brains—becomes the *mature adult sapient* of cognitive reconsideration, primed to inhibit DANE brain's lust for immediate gratification. It is easy to see how such gradations can become perverted and thus corruptive and pathological. A strong SANE brainmark is the best defense against arrogance and the rise of psychopathy.

Briefly, this vigorous brain condition originates in the *raphe nuclei,* with neurons distributed along the entire length of the brain stem. Serotonin is manufactured from a precursor amino acid, L-tryptophan, as a part of carbohydrate metabolization (a fact justifying a balanced diet of at least a 30 percent daily intake of carbohydrates). Providing adequate amino-acid precursors for the manufacture of serotonin contributes to the blooming of what we call the SANE brainmark (high-gain serotonin acts to modulate sexual and lustful influences from DANE brain's excitatory functions; in its absence, DANE brain can bully the entire brain with the pleasure molecules lying behind addictions to sex and pornography). SANE brain's serotonin liberation remains one of the most important stabilizers in preserving the adaptive versions of the 70–80 percent of the neurospectrum.

SANE brain liberation lies behind controlling ourselves, even at times when external stimuli are strong and compelling. It's not a SANE brain virtue to throw caution to the wind. When our brains become fully mature, we finally understand that all behavior is tied to consequence. A serotonin-rich brain is a central ingredient in projecting the passionate dedication to a set of principles and higher ideals characteristic of an intelligent individual absent the "salesmanship" and con artistry of those who have hidden agendas.

High-gain quantities of serotonin released along cortical pathways "mark" the brain for inhibitory control. In full power, the serotonin brainmark produces a person who is pleasantly engaging to others, projects affect (emotion) worthy of respect and leadership, embodies healthy self-esteem, and is surrounded by a calming *halo effect of trust*.

As a bonus, the liberated serotonin brain merges perfectly with a mature prefrontal cortex and the accompanying regulatory control, producing individuals perceived as calming, nonthreatening allies who are both likable and believable. Unmatched as a calming chemistry, liberated serotonin at synapse is required for rest, rejuvenation, recuperation, and sleep cycling. Tangential activities associated with serotonin elevation are mood and affect regulation, body temperature, sleep, and postcoital satiety typified by skin-on-skin bonding (aided by the hormones oxytocin and vasopressin).

Sapient brains are prone to engaging in deceptive practices because such behavior often gets liars out of trouble, at least temporarily. What could be more of an effective cognitive strategy in dodging trouble than to tell a lie? When lies still get us "grounded" as adolescents, we may discover the importance of taking our medicine by telling the truth. The evolution of SANE brain, featuring soothing serotonin, becomes our best solution: We get out of trouble by not getting into trouble in the first place—a lesson that requires years to learn.

Making decisions that steer us away from having to lie is central to PFC regulatory control, characterizing the mature, appropriate, and socially conscious pathway made possible by serotonin efficacy. Discovering the transparency of truth telling is a treasure to strive for and one of the important lessons a teenager can learn about deception. The alternative—lying—soon becomes mired in more deception and backfires on adolescents who have become compulsive liars. The mitigating excitatory agendas of DANE-PEA brainmarks require a state of constant deception crafted to dodge the truth, while the straightforward SANE brain produces the calm, cool, collected, and confident demeanor of an intelligent individual on the way to young adulthood. The ability to control one's self is a cardinal trait of adaptation. "Playing by the rules," even in instances of hard-charging ambition, is a key factor in the ability to keep behavior on an even keel from cascading serotonin.

In those with a strong SANE brain, others observe a hard-working confidence behind their achievement rather than arrogant self-entitlement. A display of SANE brain, enhanced by mature PFC regulatory control, is a prime characteristic of the adult brain. As such, the dominance of SANE brain is reflected in surviving and thriving by making smart decisions and taking all facts into consideration. Our dreams can come true with SANE brain taking the lead. Without the ability to control DANE brain, life becomes a rat race as it currently exists for many of the poor, uneducated, addicted, disenfranchised, mentally ill, and incarcerated criminals who failed to control themselves in their youth.

Raphe nuclei are a cluster of moderate-sized cells located in the brain stem whose sole function is the release of serotonin across the entire brain. This region is the target of SSRIs (selective serotonin reuptake inhibitors), a group of antidepressant medications believed to activate serotonin nuclei, producing a continual cascade of serotonin as a "mood brightener" that impacts self-esteem and confidence. Axons from raphe nuclei ascend to the cerebral cortex, the limbic system, and *basal ganglia*—deeply placed cell clusters associated with cognition, emotion, learning, and motor control. Basal ganglia, in turn, target other regional nuclei as a "striatum," with links to the dopamine-rich pathways of the *caudate nucleus* (learning and memory), *putamen* (movement and learning), and *nucleus accumbens* (pleasure, addiction, reward, laughter, and the placebo effect). Neurons from the raphe nuclei descend to the *medulla* (a region of autonomic regulatory neurons that control respiration and blood pressure) and to the spinal cord.

The SANE brain, with its chemical activator serotonin, is the interwoven brainmark linking the PFC to calm, reflective thoughts, often producing solid decisions that ultimately lead to success and happiness in both careers and relationships.

ENGAGING OUR SANE BRAIN

The vigorous brain condition characterized by high-gain serotonin and illuminated by PFC regulatory control offers the best brainmark for winning friends, influencing others, climbing career ladders, remaining calm in a gathering storm, and even winning over voters in political elections. If the serotonin brain is underdeveloped, immature, or lacking in substantial connections, the alternative is to resort to a masquerade by faking the attributes of a mature brain—a ploy that is often difficult to maintain and easily recognized and interpreted as red flags by others with strong SANE brains. The PFC and accompanying high-gain serotonin versus the midbrain limbic system—the major reward center in the mammalian brain and the brainmark most illuminated in adolescence—can now be understood as the major inhibitory-excitatory axis of the mammalian brain.

Rapid cascades of both inhibitory and excitatory chemistry flow through the PFCs of the human frontal lobes. Cocooned within twin frontal lobes that are near mirror images of each other, the prefrontal aspects include three regions of primary importance to cognitive influences, emotion, and expression of the DANE-SANE brain. Cognitive activities such as brainstorming, making plans, and problem solving come from cortices in the *dorsolateral PFC*. A critical function of the *ventromedial PFC* is merging emotional meaning with cognition, such as processing feelings that drive reward-seeking behavior. Selective attention and deciding upon which course of action to take come from cortices in the *orbitofrontal PFC*— located directly behind the forehead, between the eyes and above the nose, in essence the "dashboard" of the brain. Vital to decision making and embracing consequences, both typical of the adult brain, the PFC is the brain region most dependent upon experiences and learning during and beyond puberty, often well into middle age.

Neurocognitive mapping—the powerful thinking "maps" of experiences and perceptions that provide reference points for making good decisions in crafting solutions—is enhanced by the SANE brain's abilities to produce cool and collected confidence. This reality suggests we must "fold up the playpen and put away our toys." By doing so in young adulthood, we can more realistically address fundamental neurotruths and thus seek ways to more effectively handle the challenges of living, working, and parenting in the 21st century.

In modern life, we can expect behavioral characteristics to surface as brain conditions that must be confronted in teenagers. One obvious neurotruth suggests that parents must act as their teenager's prefrontal cortex by drawing "deep lines in the sand" relative to accountability, at least until that teenager's PFCs become more mature. Although psychological manipulation and deceptive practices are woven into the struggle for existence and bred into cortices of the brain from nature's ancient evolutionary engines, we must, whenever possible, find kernels of neurotruth to balance the scales of human drama until our progeny find "calmer waters" in the SANE brain.

From neuroscience, the conclusion is abundantly clear that we are not a dead species walking. Rather, we continually address new facts that become apparent to all of us sooner or later. For readers who are parents, ask yourself this question: Do today's adolescents appear more self-indulgent or less self-indulgent than baby boomers (born 1946–1964) when they were adolescents? Common *res ipsa* evidence—evidence anyone can determine if he or she is attentive to surroundings—often provides reliable answers far ahead of scientists who conduct research studies to prove their points.

A review of pop-culture articles from a variety of sources suggests that today's version of adolescent brains are far more self-indulgent and self-entitled than previous generations. We are not speaking of "rebels without causes" but of teenagers as a whole. The America perceived and portrayed by TV producers and directors validates behavior of the teenage and young adult masses of self-absorbed narcissists, as observed in the shows *Jersey Shore, Pretty Little Liars,* and realty programs featuring the Kardashians and various celebrities de jour. In analyzing and describing today's pop-culture adolescent behavior, we can put different shades of lipstick on this pig, but we still have the same brain—a brain addicted to stimulating and dangerous activities.

Foregoing the spin placed on life by the popular media, neurotruths—brain truths we can count on—must emerge. What better place to look for truth than neuroscience, particularly neuropsychology, now equipped with tools and products that are peering deep into cerebral landscapes with neuroscans aimed at living tissue and recorded in real time?

DANE BRAIN VERSUS SANE BRAIN

The influence of the DANE brain as initiator of "reward systems" brain-wide constitutes the most powerful, but potentially dangerous, sapient brainmark of all, especially when PEA, DHEA, and testosterone are added to this excitatory mix. Though DANE brain contributes directly to passion, focus, and motivation, and in particular to sexual varieties of passion, without regulatory control from SANE brain to modulate dopamine and norepinephrine, DANE brain can become perverted to the extent that corruptive and pathological psychopathy result. (These conditions can also occur due to cortical maladaptations, with damage to or malfunctioning of regions of the paralimbic system.) Perhaps SANE brain's most valuable contribution to Homo sapient existence is to take the edge off impulsive and empowered or entitled behavior, thereby establishing self-control through a consideration of consequences. While DANE brain promotes emotion and behavior that work best under deceptive practices (some kind of cover), the SANE brainmark moves us ever closer to transparency, speaking the truth, and living our lives in social harmony.

In contrast, when DANE brain "bullies" or dominates a weakly performing SANE brain and PFC, a scenario of arrogance arises—feelings of entitlement and empowerment of "personality," essentially giving permission to a hubristic mindset regardless of consequences. Examples of hubris can be found, for example, in the profiles of "wealth" manager Bernard

Madoff and former Illinois governor Rod Blagojevich. And news reports from around the world reveal what corruption and violence can do not only to victims but also to entire communities. No one can deny the predatory nature of our species. (The authors share the perspective of others who believe *all* crimes involve larceny—stealing something of value from others—whether it is personal property, good reputations, or lives [as in violent murder].) As our SANE brain grows in strength along with the PFC, we discover, sometimes painfully, those who may appear as such do not always have our best interests at heart.

EVERYTHING IS A CLUE

We must pay attention to behavior. It is the responsibility of every individual to see through manipulation and deceptive practices in all forms and to respond with the mature analyses of the SANE brainmark. When coupled with PFC efficacy in balancing DANE brain, the SANE brainmark helps us make hard decisions and move steadily toward our cherished dreams. We can investigate the world around us for truth and embrace the more scientific version—neurotruth.

Neurotransmitters are chemical messengers within *interneurons* (brain cells) that become activated when *vesicles* (microscopic packets within axon terminals) release molecules of specific chemistry due to an electro-chemical process known as *exocytosis.* This biological process spills endogenous chemistry into *synaptic clefts* The terminal ends of neurons, called *axons,* which contain the vesicles of transmitter molecules, release chemical "messages" that are "transmitted" to neighboring chemo-receptors called *dendrites.* Synaptic clefts are literally the "microspaces" separating axons from dendrites. Billions of transmitters make for trillions of connections in sapient brains. What happens in these connections is an axiomatic neurotruth: The chemical strength of our own varieties and variations of endogenous chemistry marks or primes our brains in slightly and, in some cases, monumental gradations. True idiosyncratic tweaks are accomplished by merging nurture's perceptual experiences into the "stewpot" of chemistry. Without strong prefrontal regulatory control (from the PFC) enhanced by a highly functioning SANE brainmark, chaos overrides human behavior via DANE brain, especially when DANE brain has been exposed to toxic parenting and peer influences.

Across the spectrum of possibilities, it is a foundational neurotruth that transmitter chemistry acting in nature's best game of adaptation produces the following characteristics: (1) the adaptive tenacity and resilience seen in survivors and thrivers, (2) amped-up varieties of passionate, ambition-driven achievers seen as society's movers and shakers, and (3) and the alphas of the species, who are innovators and world changers. Adaptive achievers comprise the lion's share of the neurospectrum (70–80 percent) of life-affirming characteristics, largely driven by the maturity of PFC regulatory control. Even the creative and highly idiosyncratic kept astute control of themselves in their moments of adversities. This achievement-oriented aspect in adaptive varieties, incorrectly referred to as "psychopathic," is far from it. It can best be summarized as the SANE brain–driven brilliance typical of overachievers who change the world with a plan and a passion.

This same chemistry, developing in the midst of *toxic milieu experiences,* must certainly be driven by unknown biological maladaptations, as well as physical traumas such as concussions and contusions of the brain. It produces the self-defeating behaviors characteristic of corruptive harmers as well as the rapaciousness of pathological psychopaths—individuals characterized as violent intraspecies predators (Hare 1993). These corruptors and violent psychopaths comprise the remaining 20–30 percent of the spectrum and are correctly called "psychopaths," delighting in their supreme maladaptation while possessing neither conscience nor empathy.

Due to daily interactions between excitatory and inhibitory chemistry, our brainmarks shuffle back and forth in efficacy, depending upon external stimuli, internal scheming, or on-the-fly motivations. Waxing and waning pathways characterized by chemical activators such as SANE brain (driven by the inhibitory neurotransmitter serotonin) and DANE brain (driven by excitatory dopamine, norepinephrine, and PEA) prime us for our obsessions, compulsions, and private desires. This teeter-totter of affect and cognition (thinking) is modulated across longer periods of time by *second messenger transmission,* so the quality of our cognition is of utmost importance in this regard.

THE GENERATION GAP: A MATTER OF INCHES

The serotonin brain gives us the tenacity and resilience to embrace reality and solve life's problems. A cool, calm, collected, and confident affect and cognition from SANE brain embrace truth and make decisions based upon careful analysis. By contrast, DANE brain, ever chasing pleasurable and near-irresistible chemical fixes from eating, sex, and human drama, paints a completely different perception—one coated in hedonistic and narcissistic tactics tailored toward deceptive practices. DANE brain is not a "thinking brain" as much as an "experimenting, emotive and impulsive, and sexual brain." In contrast, adults nearing 30 to 40 years of age live a majority of the time well connected to the PFC—the region most influenced by personal experiences. So a neurotruth to live by is the realization that parents and adolescents rarely communicate with each other from the same brain regions. A true "generation gap" exists between adult and adolescent brains. Brain-wise, parents and their progeny are about two inches or less away from the dominant brains: PFC for adults and MLS for adolescents. The chances are slim they will agree on anything.

In adolescence, the excitatory DANE brain reinforces impulsivity and pushing boundaries, forever meeting resistance from the parental, inhibitory SANE brain. This cortical "grudge match" between parent and child will last approximately 12 to 15 years, starting at about age 13 and running its developmental course by age 25 to 27 (longer in some cases). A study by neuroscientist Jay Giedd illustrates that the brain develops in a progression from bottom to top then back to front. As a result, regions of the adult brain, especially the prefrontal cortex, are last in the developmental line and most dependent on everyday experiences to become fully illuminated and thus strongly connected.

When illuminated, the SANE brain via liberated serotonin characterizes the mature and prosocial adult brain—the brain highlighted by prefrontal regulatory control within the frontal lobes of the brain. With low-gain serotonin, no inhibitory "mood modulator" exists to aid in the control of the adolescent obsession for immediacy and impulsivity. The importance of illuminating the serotonin pathway toward brain-wide influences cannot be overstated. Without the mature decision-making capability of the adult brain, we would have no civilization, no responsibility tied to consequence, no professionalism, no higher ideals, philosophy, and neuroscience. If truth is a temperature, it is cool and analytical, not hot and calculating.

THE LAME-SANE BRAIN

In low-gain scarcity, all cascading neurotransmitter chemistries have steep downsides. Low-gain serotonin can fuel a furious appetite for aggression and violent behavior and operate as a fuse to eating disorders, low self-esteem, the drive to self-medicate, and, ultimately, addiction and violence. A neurotruth of investigative neuroscience is that low-gain serotonin, in the presence of high testosterone efficacy, produces fierce arrogance and aggression; when it is mixed with frustration and anger, violence is typically observed, especially in cold-blooded psychopathic criminal minds.

A lame SANE brain (in low-gain scarcity) up against raging testosterone efficacy was dramatically documented in the case of Cornell University graduate Michael Ross, who claimed responsibility for murdering eight young women. High levels of testosterone, the hormone of aggression and libido, pitted against a low-gain SANE brainmark produced a dangerous imbalance (most surely exacerbated by deviant cognitive mapping), resulting in his garishly violent crimes. Diagnosed with *sexual sadism,* Ross compared his violent sexual urges to "living with an obnoxious roommate I could not escape." While incarcerated for multiple homicides against the young women, all of them strangers, he was given Depo-Provera (a testosterone blocker) in an effort to lower his surging levels, a measure mandated to protect female prison guards. When his low-gain serotonin brain could no longer be "bullied" by surging testosterone, a marked change in Ross's attitude occurred. As his serotonin brainmark gradually gained strength over lowered testosterone, he began writing articles concerning his dramatic "personality" change, warning others of the dangers of out-of-control chemical imbalances. He claimed he felt normal—and remorseful—for the first time in his life; as a result, he did not challenge his death penalty, a consequence he felt he deserved.

A particularly devastating side effect of *serotonin scarcity* is the tendency for afflicted individuals to self-medicate in an attempt to anesthetize depersonalized feelings (low self-esteem, anxiety, or over-aggressiveness) with alcohol or other drugs. This leads to intoxication from a variety of sources firing up DA spikes and cascades within the midbrain limbic system, a region capable of being saturated with dopaminergic neurons (neurons stimulated by dopamine). It is thought that adolescents who experiment with drugs are attempting to self-medicate in hopes of eradicating fear, anxiety, and low self-esteem, all analogues of the lame SANE brain. Quick highs from illegal drugs such as cocaine and marijuana transition the DANE brain into the dominant brainmark, even more so with immature prefrontal regulatory control. Constant "hits" from the drug of choice produce "fat and sassy" dopamine neurons resistant to being pruned back in adolescence and young adulthood.

Nature and nurture are always in the picture of fluctuating and modulating chemistry and hormones, depending upon genetics and social influences. Not everyone is born with exactly the same levels (or chemical "set points") of serotonin, dopamine, or any of the other chemical brainmarks. Why some brains are more sensitive to chemical activators (exciters) and inhibitors (modulators) remains a mystery. Yet the importance of family and peer milieu influences upon genetics (levels of neurochemistry in the synapses, for example) cannot be ignored and remain important in research. The best answer may be a combination of genetics and social learning that are often difficult to qualify to a certainty. At the end of the day, the spectrum reminds us that people are not exactly the same. Individuals are indeed like proverbial snowflakes—genetics, experiences, and learning all affect idiosyncratically who we are at any given moment.

GABA AND BETA-ENDORPHIN

Gamma-aminobutyric acid, the major inhibitory neurotransmitter in the CNS, provides a strong counterbalance against the effects of glutamate, the major excitatory neurotransmitter. GABA's *anxiolytic* properties, which mitigate anxiety and enhance and complement the high-gain SANE brain, are further enhanced by endorphinergic neurons within beta-endorphin pathways, providing soothing analgesic and anesthetic effects as the beta-endorphin brainmark. These chemical transmitters are interdisciplinary partners that coalesce to boost the powerful SANE brain—one of the most vital and vigorous brain conditions in our struggle for existence.

The GABA brain produces feelings of tranquility by mitigating anxiety, while the beta-endorphin brain acts as an analgesic. High-gain beta-endorphin lies behind the "runner's high" known to follow physical exertion. Like serotonin, GABA acts as an "off switch," decreasing the likelihood an excitatory signal (like DANE) will tip the brain's balance of power. Similar to the conditions of SANE brain, the chemistry of GABA calms as a natural CNS tranquilizer with properties that induce sleep and buffer aggression.

An integral function of GABA is the prevention of hyperstimulation throughout the CNS by mitigating the effects of its antagonist, *glutamate.* The GABA-glutamate axis of inhibitory versus excitatory jazzers aligns GABA and glutamate on a chemical seesaw as the major workhorses of the brain in much the same fashion as SANE brain versus DANE brain. Interestingly, glutamate receptors outnumber GABA receptors almost two to one. The two most populated neurotransmitter sites in the CNS, receptors for these core chemicals are generally dispersed throughout the brain, in contrast to the *monoamines* (dopamine, norepinephrine, and serotonin) and *acetylcholine,* which perform specialized modulating functions and are often confined to specific regions and structures of the brain.

Glutamate plays a role in *adaptive neuroplasticity,* allowing for on-the-fly cortical "rewiring." Learning and memory are activated by excitatory receptivity primarily in the hippocampus of the limbic system. Where would students be without memory?

With chemical liberation of GABA, the high-gain GABA brain elicits a feeling of inner calm and tranquility. GABA scarcity at synapse, on the other hand, is the culprit for feeling anxiety. Ever mindful of the continuum present in the neurospectrum from vigorous brain conditions, anxiety occurs as a reaction to perceived stress. To combat GABA deficiency at synapse, Xanax, a drug that works by blocking GABA reuptake and thereby increases synaptic liberation, is often prescribed. Most recently, neural activity in the amygdala and hippocampus have arisen as suspects in the appearance of anxiety. PET (positron emission tomography) scans—high-resolution imaging of the brain—show increased blood flow to the amygdala when moderate anxiety is experienced.

THE HIGH-GAIN GABA BRAINMARK

With a high-gain GABA brain, we feel wonderfully tranquil and worry-free; it's easy to see how this brainmark, coupled with SANE brain, leads to a peaceful, calming effect and the appearance of a laid-back and easygoing confidence to others. Add to this mix a high-gain endorphin brain and a sense of well-being radiates.

Endorphins, the best-known family of *endogenous opioid peptides,* are controlled by the hypothalamus and produced in the pituitary glands for body-wide effects via hormones—the chemical messengers of the bloodstream. Endorphins produce *analgesia,* working wonders as natural pain killers. Discovered in the 1970s, the endogenous opioid peptide and neurotransmitter beta-endorphin is found in the hypothalamus and pituitary glands, exerting powerful effects in both the central and peripheral nervous systems. It is an agonist of opioid receptors, with evidence suggesting it serves as the endogenous *ligand* (ions or molecules that bind to chemical receptors of the M-opioid receptor), the same receptor to which the chemicals extracted from opium, morphine, and codeine find affinity. Beta-endorphinergic receptors lie behind the so-called runner's high, the body's counteractive response to the pain signals of long-distance running, flooding the brain with soothing beta-endorphin. Such liberation at synapse produces the high-gain endorphin brain, characterized by a sense of well-being, reduction of pain, easing of emotional distress, increase in self-esteem, and sense of euphoria.

Mimicking the neural effects of endorphins, opioids are natural, semi-synthetic (oxycodone and heroin) and synthetic substances (methadone) that act pharmacologically like morphine, the primary active constituent of the opium poppy. Opiates act not only on the central structures of the reward pathways via the ventral tegmental area and nucleus accumbens, but also on other structures that are naturally modulated by endorphins. These structures include the amygdala, the *locus coeruleus,* the *arcuate nucleus,* and the *periaqueductal gray matter,* which also influence dopamine levels. Opiates also affect the *thalamus*—the doorway to the cerebral cortex—which further enhances analgesic effects and fosters a sense of well-being.

Just as natural receptors exist for endogenous chemistry, similar exogenous drugs activate the same receptors with powerful efficacy, ultimately leading to addiction. The illegal drug heroin mimics the action of these endorphins, an effect that accounts for its popularity as a recreational drug. With frequent use, the constant barrage of chemistry hitting endogenous receptors causes them to thicken, thus further priming these receptors for addiction and making that addiction increasingly difficult to overcome. Continuous and sustained use of heroin for as little as three days triggers withdrawal symptoms when use is stopped abruptly, a result produced in a much shorter time frame than with other common painkillers, such as oxycodone and hydrocodone.

In conclusion, it is easy to see how central serotonin, GABA, and beta-endorphin are essential to our collective sanity and well-being. They lie behind our wondrous abilities to experience calm, cool, and collected confidence, which fires up abundant self-esteem by mitigating anxiety and painful emotional experiences. A life in chemical balance is a life worth living. Elizabeth Arden possessed such brainmarks, allowing her to redefine female beauty with her Red Door boutiques and scientific grasp of cosmetics. And possessing the patience of the SANE brain allowed Jaycee Dugard to survive 18 years in the grasp of a pedophile. Even in her darkest hours, she possessed the willpower and hope she would be reunited someday with those who truly loved her.

MAKING THE CASE FOR THE DIFFERENTLY-ABLED I: ELIZABETH ARDEN (1884–1966)

Elizabeth Arden

adaptive	passionate achiever	maladaptive
survivors	thrivers	corruptive	pathological

Born Florence Nightingale Graham in Ontario, Canada, Elizabeth Arden dropped out of nursing school and relocated to New York City, where she worked for Squibb Pharmaceuticals as a bookkeeper. She found, however, that she favored lab experiments over office duties, and she spent hours in Squibb labs learning all she could about skin care (*Encyclopedia Britannica*, 15th ed., s.v. "Elizabeth Arden").

At age 25, Arden formed a partnership with beauty culturist Elizabeth Hubbard. The partnership soon dissolved, but it gave Arden half the business name that would be her legacy: Elizabeth Arden, a cross between the name of her former business partner and Alford Lord Tennyson's narrative poem "Enoch Arden." At 28, Arden traveled to France to learn facial massage techniques from Parisian beauty salons and brought back to North America a collection of powders and rouges she created in those salons. She introduced modern eye makeup and the salon "makeover."

All of Arden's salons featured red doors. Having redefined what it meant to be female, Arden was one of the richest women in the world at the peak of her career. She even created the famed lipstick Montezuma Red for women in the armed forces, a shade that perfectly matched the red on their uniforms. By 1940, it was reported "only three American names are known in very single corner of the globe: Singer (for sewing machines), Coca-Cola, and Elizabeth Arden. In many ways, Arden qualifies as the female Steve Jobs as an innovator and world changer.

MAKING THE CASE FOR THE DIFFERENTLY-ABLED II: JAYCEE LEE DUGARD (1980–)

Jaycee Lee Dugard
survivor, thriver, achiever

```
adaptive                                                  maladaptive
|_____|_____|
survivors     thrivers            corruptive          pathological
```

The saga of Jaycee Lee Dugard, who fell into the hands of a sadistic pedophile, is one of the most compelling stories of hope, love, and survival. At the age of 11, Jaycee was abducted on her way to a bus stop by Phillip Garrido, then 40 years of age. Over the next 18 years, Garrido held Dugard captive, repeatedly raping her and often videotaping the brutal attacks; ultimately he would father her two children. Garrido's accomplice and wife, Nancy, who was 35 years old at the time of Dugard's kidnapping, frequently participated in the crimes as a compliant co-offender. Garrido kept his prey in one of the outbuildings on his property. Although he was a registered sex offender, investigators who searched his home in required visits never once searched the back of his property.

At his 2011 sentencing, Garrido, then over 60 years of age, received 431 years to life in prison for his crimes. The Eldorado County (California) superior court judge who pronounced the sentence said Garrido "lacked a soul" and called his actions "beyond horrible" (*New York Times,* June 2, 2011). His wife Nancy, then 55, was sentenced to 36 years to life; she cannot be paroled until she is over 70. Those attending the sentencing witnessed the cold stare of Garrido, clearly a pathological psychopath (exacerbated most likely by a dual diagnosis of periodic schizophrenia). As is common with most grandiosely arrogant psychopaths, nothing in his countenance during the proceedings suggested an ounce of remorse.

Jaycee Dugard possessed the brain chemistry to become a tenacious and resilient survivor and thriver, a tenacity expressed by her hope and her love for her two children. She had made up her mind that someday she would be reunited with her family and openly forgave the Garridos for what they did to her, stating that she harbors no resentment for her childhood being so viciously stolen. What an amazing example of the power of hope and love.

Chapter 7

Neuroglia, the Paralimbic System, and the "Gut"

READERS' PRE-TEST

The neuron doctrine thoroughly explains how endogenous neurochemistry produces brainmarks. True or false?

The answer is false.

There exists a "brain" in the gut. True or false?

The answer is true.

The paralimbic system has been shown to be good place to start when searching for the answers to psychopathy at the tissue level. True or false?

The answer is true.

ONCE HIDDEN AND NOW FUTURE BRAIN

It is our goal for the four chapters in part 2 of our book to offer breakthrough discoveries in the science of the brain chemistry that lie behind adaptive and restorative chemistry as well as the chemistry of corruptive and pathological psychopathy. To that end, we now address *neuroglia,* the discovery of which has put a dent in the long-standing efficacy of the *neuron doctrine.* As R. Douglas Fields (2011b) notes, "Our understanding of the brain was based on a century-old idea: *the neuron doctrine.* But this theorem is deeply flawed. . . . Flashy neurons may get the attention, but a class of cells called glia are behind most of the brain's work—and many of its diseases. . . . Unlike neurons which communicate across chains of synapses, glia broadcast their signal widely, like cell phones."

Once considered mere "packing material" configured around neurons like cotton candy, the significance of neuroglia (or, simply, glia) is today better understood. New insights show deficiencies can now be pursued in the neuroglia rather than relying, as we have done for decades, solely upon dictates from the *neuron doctrine.* Thus far, we have made the same argument regarding the role of psychopathy relative to the neurospectrum, that is, maladaptive versions—corruptive and pathological perversions of the neurospectrum producing what the world calls psychopathy—accounting for approximately 20 to 30 percent of the neurospectrum. In contrast, the lion's share—70 to 80 percent, equivalent to the power of neuroglia's brain-wide influence—represents the best in adaptive brain conditions. Along with excitatory chemistry, inhibitory chemistry, and blood-messenger hormones, the "hidden brain" of neuroglia, the paralimbic system, and our "gut" contribute to the strengths of life-affirming chemistry. In this chapter, we argue that the neuroglia, the paralimbic system, and our gut offer a more complete story of how life-affirming chemistry, if perverted in narcissism and arrogance, can be destructive.

First, it is instructive to mention a few words about the neuron doctrine. This paradigm proposed that the CNS worked by electrical impulses occurring in neurons releasing endogenous neurochemistry (neurotransmitters such as dopamine, norepinephrine, and serotonin) as chemical cascades into microspaces from tiny sacs called vesicles. Due to exocytosis, vesicles "dissolved apart" from stimuli involved in perception—vision, touch, smell, taste, and hearing—resulting in molecules of transmitters spilling into the microspaces, where they bonded to targeted receptors on neighboring cells. By this process, vigorous brain conditions were activated, including pleasure, euphoria, depression, as well as so-called chemical imbalances producing "mental disorders." Centrally implicated in order and disorder were DANE brain's *dopaminergic* cells or SANE brain's *serotonergic* cells, specifically with messages to "chill" or reconsider.

This neurobehavioral paradigm became supported by the medical model of disorder, dysfunction, and disease as "chemical imbalances," which were theorized to occur in synapses with excitatory versus inhibitory chemistry that marked the brain. Suddenly, biological psychiatry saw a way to become wealthy. What resulted amounted to a medical collusion between clinical psychiatrists and big pharmaceutical companies. What has evolved, of course, is the common practice today of disease mongering—"peddling" prescriptive medications for "diseases" (chemical imbalances). Some imbalances were attributed to serotonin imbalances producing depression or GABA scarcity producing anxiety, while others were more obscure, such as spectrum autism, "restless leg syndrome," social anxiety disorder, adult ADD, and something called "body dysmorphic disorder" (which causes the sufferer to believe the ears or nose, for example, are out of portion to the face). This presumptive alliance prompted the prescription of legal drugs to return the patient to chemical balance. This approach has proven to be fundamentally wrongheaded, a *res ipsa* conclusion from observation of a flood of side effects due to concentration on the wrong mechanisms—neurons instead of neuroglia and the gut. Who knew, at the time, the wrong mechanism was being "preyed upon" by greedy and narcissistic practitioners?

THE HIDDEN BRAIN COMES ALIVE

Known functions of several types of neuroglia have allowed neuroscientists to tell a more complete story of how vigorous sapient brains work and how psychopathy figures into the spectrum as a major maladaptation. According to R. Douglas Fields, author of *The Other Brain* (2011b), "*Glial cells* (neuroglia or glia) make up 85% of the cells of sapient brains and, unlike neurons, are the *real powerhouses of cerebral activities.*"

What we know today contradicts how prescriptive meds were theorized to work, that is, by regulating transmitter levels entering synapses and connecting to receptors. No wonder there existed and continues to exist so many troubling side effects. Now we know that job belongs to *astrocytes*—a subtype of neuroglia. Prior to this breakthrough, psychoactive medications were created to block (diminish chemistry) or block reuptake (increase) levels of a targeted neurotransmitter such as dopamine. Astrocytes were not known at that time as the agent of controlling synapses. Therefore, by targeting the wrong mechanisms—neurotransmitter levels in the synaptic gaps—a multitude of the prescribed drugs' side effects skyrocketed, explaining the common occurrence today of drugs often making conditions far worse. So today, new experimental drugs are directed toward astrocytes.

New research shows our sapient brains are far more superior in communication protocols due to glial cells than were once explained by the neuron doctrine. For instance, some information bypasses neurons completely, flowing without the electrical charge through networks of glia (Fields 2011a, 54). So new insights from neuroglia research suggest only 15 percent of neurons make up our brain cells, while glial cells make up the lion's share and more fully explain the human condition of neurological and psychological adaptation versus maladaptation. New research has also uncovered glia's central role in the processing of new information and how glia, at times, interact with neurons by cooperating or, at other times, controlling or creating possibilities for maladaptation. For instance, aging glial cells can disintegrate and signal dementia. For sure, glia cells are certainly more than the "glue" once thought to surround neurons in supportive roles only by "holding" together cerebral tissue. Not knowing the functional roles of neuroglia led psychiatry into its corruptive alliance with pharmaceutical companies. We are reminded of the timely quote from medical toxicologist Alan Hall, MD (2009): "I have cured more patients by taking them off medication than by putting them on meds."

NEUROGLIA: DIFFERENTLY-ABLED COMMUNICATORS

Specialized neuroglia—the *oligodendrocytes* (cells with a few branches), the sausage-shaped *Schwann cells,* and the star-shaped *astrocytes*—none of which are configured with recognizable structures, are common to neurons such as axons, dendrites, or synapses. *Oligodendrocytes* produce myelin sheath—a fatty substance creating a layer of insulation around neurons in the CNS—by wrapping around axons, creating the recognizable "white matter" function to the transmission of impulses in the CNS. Neurons without myelin are known as "gray matter." The Schwann cells manufacture myelin for use in the *peripheral nervous system* (PNS). Also, Schwann cells help control muscle contractions.

As it is now known, neuroglia are just differently-abled communicators doing vital jobs in cerebral hemispheres, while all these years hiding in plain sight. Before the proliferation of new glial research, astrocytes—another type of neuroglia—were once theorized to transport nutrients to neurons and carry waste products away in "janitorial" fashion. That all changed with new (and ongoing) research; neuroscientists now understand that neurons are highly dependent on astrocytes and other glia cells for firing impulses as both glial cells and neurons share neurotransmitters. Also, astrocytes provide biochemical support for the *endothelial cells* forming the blood-brain barrier, providing nutrients to tissues, maintaining the extracellular ion balance, and performing a "reparatory function" in the brain and spinal cord following trauma.

As it turned out, neuroglia were participating in cerebral communication and "talking" among themselves without benefit of electrical impulses. The tools for discovery of how electricity worked in neurons could not detect the activity of neuroglia. However, as mentioned previously, when "tracer dyes" came into common use in the 1980s and 1990s, the significance of glial cells appearing as "flashes of light" (detected by present-day video and laser-illuminated microscopes) was discovered. (The dyes were able to reflect calcium ions, which caused the dye to generate light. As neurons were stimulated to fire, the surrounding glial cells also became activated with neurotransmitters, evidenced by glowing calcium.) Not only were glia communicating with neurons, but using this tool, scientists discovered glial cells were communicating with each other and releasing the same neurotransmitter as that cascading from surrounding neurons.

Hence, neuroglia provides nonelectrical pathways for cortical "talk" widely across the brain (like cell phones), just as neurons provide electrochemical versions as next-door neighbors. Neurons communicate rapidly in thousandths of a second, while glia communicate more slowly in seconds or tens of seconds (Fields 2011a, 56), thereby activating and modulating neuronal messages across extended time frames.

GLIAL CELLS AND ILLNESSES

Glial cells are major players in neurological and psychological illnesses, ranging from epilepsy to chronic pain and depression (Fields 2011a, 57). Again, neurons alone were once theorized to be the culprits for imbalances, disorder, disease, and dysfunction. Today, neuroglia—particularly *microglia*—have been implicated as major defenders against disease (Fields 2011a, 57), as microglia and astrocytes seek out and destroy invading germs and other agents of destruction while aiding in recovery from disease by releasing healing chemistry. How radical is this theory? If the healthy body with its strong immune system is simply left alone to heal itself, it will do so, as such chemistry makes for remarkable adaptation. Using drugs exacerbates the situation by adding life-threatening side effects, which are, according to the 2006 film *Big Bucks, Big Pharma: Marketing Disease and Pushing Drugs,* the fifth leading cause of death in America (Media Education Foundation 2006).

Microglia are chemical scavengers in the CNS seeking out plaques and infections to chemically neutralize as well as absorbing and repairing damaged neurons; if not for microglia, infectious agents and foreign bodies would cross the blood-brain barrier and in the process destroy sensitive neural tissue, perhaps the entire brain itself. Microglia are one of the most sensitive agents in the body, making remarkably small pathological changes in the CNS and functioning best in emergencies. That neuroglia would play such as central role in neurological disease follows logic, as they are the body's first responders to disease.

We have long known that *demyelinating disorders* such as multiple sclerosis strip away myelin from axons, causing the disease's crippling symptoms. This has convinced some scientists that Alzheimer's disease might result from microglia having lost the ability to clear cellular wastes. Normally, microglia is expected to surround and "swallow" toxic proteins forming *amyloid plaques*. The very same process appears to ease chronic pain. Today, we know that malfunctioning glial cells account for the experience of chronic pain as well as the diminishing the power of medications. Pharmacologists are now targeting neuroglia rather than neurons in recent animal studies in the treatment of chronic and debilitating pain.

Also, the analysis of brain tissue postmortem links oligodendrocytes and astrocytes to depression and schizophrenia (Fields 2011a, 58). New research and awareness of the role played by neuroglia suggest pharmacological treatment in the future will be targeting glia rather than neurons for relief from epilepsy and sleep disorders (59). From new laser tools and video imaging, breakthrough insights have emerged as we can now demarcate between glial and neuronal influences as differently-abled components of the CNS (and PNS), leading to our amazing "special weapons and tactics" centered on adaptation. When neuroglia becomes maladaptive, it is *res ipsa* evident that "all hell can break loose," including characteristics of corruptive and violent behavior, better known as psychopathy.

> The most mysterious substance on earth is the stuff between your ears, and much of the intrigue exists because many long-held beliefs about how the brain works have turned out to be wrong.

(Fields 2011a, 54)

THE RING OF FIRE: THE PARALIMBIC SYSTEM

More directly in line with our topic—psychopathy—what can we learn from a quick scan of the region of the brain known as the paralimbic system? If an internal brain compass existed, the readings on the dial of the compass when placed in the exact center of the limbic system (located just above the midbrain) would show the parameters of cerebral tissue in four directions of the paralimbic system—a neurological site that features structures that may give rise to psychopathic characteristics we have identified as corruptive and violent psychopathy. There is some accumulating evidence that the midbrain limbic system, comprising influences from the midbrain per se and the limbic system per se when connected minimally, partially, or when damaged by trauma, can result in the perversion of adaptation leading to maladaptive perversion and can become the breeding ground for the realization of arrogance in corruptive psychopathy and grandiose arrogance in pathological psychopathy. This 21st-century insight is bolstered by functional magnetic resonance imaging (fMRI) scans of these regions showing the diminished blood flow indicative of damage or maladaptation.

Geographically, the northernmost segment (upward) of our imaginary compass reaches the entire top of the *corpus callosum*—the "hard-body" bundle of tissue connecting the right hemisphere to the left hemisphere, located in the exact center of the brain. The eastern segment (toward posterior cortices of the brain) is the occipital lobe, known to activate sight. The western segment (forward into anterior regions of the frontal lobes just above our eyes) is the all-important PFC. Finally, the southernmost segment extends downward into the temporal lobes and encapsulates the amygdala. The facts most encouraging about this "ring of psychopathy" is what each structure is known to initiate but in failure produces instead: maladaptation or what clinicians persist in calling disorders.

What follows is a quick overview of the anterior aspects of the paralimbic region's neurons and neuroglia that produce vigorous brain conditions:

- When healthy and adaptive, the anterior cingulate is the cortical site for decision making, empathy, and affect; when maladaptive, dysfunction can be observed in the failure of empathy and blunted affect—two characteristics measured on the PCL-R.
- When healthy and adaptive, the orbitofrontal PFC is known as the "dashboard" of the brain and the "last tollbooth" for the expression of cognitive reconsideration. The orbitofrontal PFC is critical in decision making, impulse control, and opportunities (or not) for behavioral flexibility. In maladaptation, applying consequences from learning is severely limited (yet another trait measured by the PCL-R).
- When healthy and adaptive, the ventromedial PFC merges feelings with cognitive "brainstorming," thus producing excellent options for action; in contrast, and in instances of maladaptation, affect (emotion) becomes inappropriately

expressed in, for example, smiles at inappropriate times—again often observed in psychopathy.

Below are some instances of adaptation versus maladaptation in posterior paralimbic regions:

- When adaptive and healthy, the posterior cingulate produces emotional processing connected to emotional memory; in maladaptation, affect becomes blunted as actions become disconnected from memory.
- When adaptive and healthy, the insula alerts mind to pain perception; in maladaptation, a high tolerance to pain is observed.
- When adaptive and healthy, the temporal lobe integrates emotion, perception, and the social interactional cues necessary for collaboration; in maladaptation, empathy disintegrates, becoming disconnected from social cues and producing inappropriate behavior.
- When adaptive and healthy, the amygdala is the alarm system of the brain; in contrast, maladaptation produces narcissism, entitlement, and a sense of empowerment to do whatever one desires, including taking one's life in the toxic expression of corruption and violence.

In the age of brain-imaging studies, it's no wonder paralimbic regions have become central to the neurological understanding of corruptive and violent psychopathy.

THE "BRAIN" IN THE GUT

Now we embrace the *microbiome*—the collective name for bacteria in the gut. According to John Bienenstock of McMaster University in Hamilton, Ontario, "In just the last few years, evidence has mounted from studies of rodents that gut microbiome can influence neural development, brain chemistry, and a wide range of behavioral phenomenon, including emotional behavior, pain perception, and how the stress system alarm responds in the CNS. When the balance between beneficial versus disease-causing bacteria in an animal's gastrointestinal track is tweaked, brain chemistry is likewise affected."

The brain itself can exert influences on gut bacteria, causing a vulnerability to infectious diseases. Might beneficial bacteria—known as *probiotics*—be used to treat affective disorders such as depression and anxiety? Might chronic gastrointestinal disorders from abnormal gut microbiota influence the appearance of emotional disorders, asks Siri Carpenter, author of "That Gut Feeling" (Carpenter 2012, 51). Until all of this "gut stuff" is worked out by neuroscience, we have a lot to be excited about. For some time, the human gut has been referred to as the "second brain." Incredibly, according to Carpenter, the "gut is the only organ to boast its own independent nervous system—a network of one hundred million neurons embedded in the gut wall." When the *vagus nerve*—the primary connector of the gut and the brain—is severed, the network remains functioning independently. So as we grow and develop, going from having a sterile gut at birth to eventually having our own "stewpot" of bacterial species consisting of one hundred trillion microbes, our GI tract transforms into a microbe playground critical to health (gut bacteria also regulate digestion and metabolism)" (ibid., 52).

MAKING THE CASE FOR THE DIFFERENTLY-ABLED I: SARA BLAKELY (1971–)

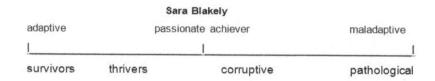

In 2000, at age 29, Sara Blakely, the daughter of a lawyer and artist, founded an undergarment company she named Spanx. After graduating from Florida State University with a degree in communications, she worked for a local stationery company (Danka) selling fax machines door to door. As a young businesswoman, she dressed up in her best to make a professional impression possible on her "cold" calls, yet her pantyhose were just not working due to the heat and humidity of Florida (*Encyclopedia Britannica,* 15th ed., s.v. "Sara Blakely").

So she cut out the feet portion of the hose. Investing $5,000 (her life savings), she picked up and moved to Atlanta. She began to research production deals with local manufactures, but her pitch for footless pantyhose failed to make the intended impression—until a co-owner of a production mill asked his own daughters if they would buy the radical pantyhose. They said yes, and Sara got her first order. She designed her own logo on a friend's computer, researched books for direction in creating her trademark name, and launched the product from her home.

Today, the Spanx brand is worth $1 billion. In 2012, Sara was named to the Time 100, the annual list of most influential people in the world. The irrepressible Sara Blakely can thank her differently-abled, tenacious, and innovative brain for finding a way to make bodies more presentable and professional looking, even in hot and humid weather.

MAKING THE CASE FOR THE DIFFERENTLY-ABLED II: MUHAMMAD ALI (1942–)

	Muhammad Ali		
adaptive	passionate achiever		maladaptive

survivors	thrivers	corruptive	pathological

> He who is not courageous enough to take risks will accomplish nothing in life.
>
> Muhammad Ali

Born Cassius Clay, Ali changed his name to Muhammad Ali when he converted to Islam in 1964, after winning the first of three world heavyweight boxing championships. His popularity as an Olympic and world-class athlete occurred during the golden age of heavyweight boxing—as the roughly two decades of boxing matches came to be known—almost exclusively due to Ali's histrionics and unorthodox boxing style, as well as his ability to predict the rounds for knockouts. All of his orchestrated "entertainment" took a nosedive in 1967 before being resurrected by highly entertaining matches—three with Joe Frazier (summarized below) and one with George Foreman (*Encyclopedia Britannica,* 15th ed., s.v. "Muhammad Ali").

The source of his troubles came from refusing, in 1967, to be inducted into military service due to his allegiance to Islam and his personal opposition to the Vietnam War. He was eventually stripped of his Olympic medals, championship titles, and permission to profit from boxing matches, only to have them returned and his boxing status reinstated by the Supreme Court of the United States.

Tall, good looking, and charming, a "gift of gab" was perhaps his most alluring trait, other than his abilities as an elite athlete. Ali was idolized by fans worldwide, due in part to several noteworthy matches—three with Ken Norton, three with Joe Frazier, and a single match with George Foreman. Match one with Frazier, the "Fight of the Century" in Madison Square Garden (1971), was won by Frazier; the second Frazier fight, a nontitle match (by then Frazier had lost his title to George Foreman) billed as "Ali-Frazier II" (January 1974), was won by Ali in a unanimous decision; and the final match, the "Thrilla in Manila," which took place in the Philippines (October 1975) and was marketed with a famous one-liner from Ali, who said the fight would be "a killa and a chilla, and a thrilla, when I get the gorilla in Manila," was won by Ali when Frazier failed to answer the bell in the 15th round.

One year earlier, Ali had engineered one of the biggest upsets in boxing history by defeating world champion George Forman in a match in Kinshasa, Zaire (today the Republic of the Congo), known as the "Rumble in the Jungle" (October 1974). This fight, among Ali's greatest, was the subject of the Academy Award–winning documentary film *When We Were Kings* (1996). In 1993, the Associated Press reported that Ali was tied with Babe Ruth as the most recognized athlete, alive or dead, in America. Ali's daughter, Laila Ali, became a champion boxer herself, even though her famous father opposed it.

In 1984, Ali was diagnosed with dementia pugilistica, a form of Parkinson's disease most likely initiated by his sport's focus on knockouts caused by violent "head shots." In June 2007, Ali received an honorary doctorate of humanities at Princeton University's 260th commencement exercises.

Chapter 8

Two Puberties and What Men Know without Knowing

READERS' PRE-TEST

In terms of gender, it does not matter what we are born—male or female—it only matters how we are raised. A male can be raised to be a female with corrective surgery. True or False?

The answer is false.

INFANTILE PUBERTY

According to Brizendine (2010), *infantile puberty* pertains to a 24 month period in which an infant girl's ovaries begin producing large amounts of estrogen to cascade through her brain and body, prompting development of her ovaries and brain regions for reproductive purposes. (The same process works in male babies with cascading testosterone, prompting genital and brain development to be accomplished at puberty.) Likewise, it triggers the growth of neurons, wiring cortical scripts for observation, communication, "gut feelings," and nurturing—tending to the care of others. By age two and a half, infantile puberty ends and the juvenile stage begins (Brizendine 2010, 19).

At a very young age, the seeds are planted for sociability and, ultimately, fertility. Stress hormones (such as cortisol) affect female progeny in deleterious ways. Moms-to-be must understand how important remaining calm, cool, and collected is during pregnancy (by manifesting the chemistry of the SANE brain with liberated serotonin), especially those who know in advance they are going to have a baby girl.

Harmonious relationships by virtue of communication and compromise punctuate brain conditions driven by estrogen-rich brains. The female's brain condition emphasizes connection and communication; by comparison, competition, often by means of aggression through sexual expression and territoriality, drives the male brain condition. Again, the testosterone cascade through the brain is pivotal in producing the male version, directly affecting the proliferation of Wolffian ducts during *embryogenesis.* As testosterone activates androgen receptors, it directs intracellular signals connecting the efferent ducts of the testes and the *epididymis, vas deferens,* and *seminal vesicles*—the outer and inner plumbing of male sexuality.

We also know that men have two and a half times the brain space devoted to sexual drive in their hypothalamus. Sexual thoughts flicker in the background of a man's visual cortex seemingly day and night, making him ready for seizing sexual opportunities. In colloquial terms, females don't always realize that a man's penis has a mind of its own. Interestingly, once a man's love and lust circuits are in sync, he falls in love, head over heels, just as a woman—perhaps even more so. Levels of estrogen and testosterone remain low during childhood (the juvenile years) for both boys and girls. The relative quiescence of this stage is the hormonal equivalent of the "calm before the storm," before puberty's tsunami of brain sexualization.

As juveniles, girls are known for "pretend games" and activities that require taking turns and encouraging and sustaining verbal volleys between friends. By contrast, boys exhibit "rough-and-tumble" play, priming brain regions for competition relative to rank, power, territory, and physical strength (Brizendine 2010, 24). That rough-and-tumble play slowly translates into workplace competition, attesting to the constant male drive to rise in the ranks of his chosen profession. Often by "hook or crook," he maneuvers, manipulates, and watches for vulnerability in others. He is less interested in connecting, unless it benefits him, and more interested in competing for the attention of those already in power. He is driven to align with those possessing influence and is sure that actions speak louder than words; in his mind, he feels he is communicating all the time via his chosen behavior.

Males also have larger brain centers for muscular action and aggression. Starting at puberty, his brain circuits for mate protection and territorial defense are hormonally primed for action. Pecking order and hierarchy matter more deeply to men than most women realize. In addition, men have larger processors in the core of the most primitive area of the brain—the amygdala—which registers fear and triggers aggression. This is why some men will fight to the death defending their loved ones.

FEMALE ADOLESCENT BRAIN CONDITIONS

The transition from a girl's juvenile stage (approximately 3 to 11 years of age) into the most disruptive stage imaginable, the *female adolescent pubescent stage* (approximately age 12 to early 20s), will test, down to the last neuron, the sanity of parents. Practically overnight, pubescent females become edgy, self-absorbed, and inclined to take risks. Although she lights up in the presence of charming males, the female may become nearly combative when her parents try to discourage such a union. Routinely, the sweet and cooperative juvenile daughter of just a few years ago is now willing to throw everybody in the household under the bus to get what she wants—her deliciously delectable charmer. She is narcissistic, feels entitled, and is primed for deceptive practices; she will lie and cover up behavior when absent from parental supervision. She ignores parental warnings in favor of her own desires, leading with her female brain, a brain both ancient and modernized in ways neuroscientists are now coming to understand. In adolescence, risk-taking behavior escalates in both male and female brains as the relative compliance of the juvenile stage gives way to the most disruptive developmental stage imaginable—pubescence intermingled in the adolescent stage.

As a condition of puberty, imagine neurons that are simultaneously engaged in high-gain proliferation while actively pruning back seldom used connections in the midst of modular reorganizing and restructuring. In short, there is a swirling dervish of brain conditions, not unlike physical binging and purging, so that every social situation can be sometimes irritating, sometimes stimulating. Welcome to the brain conditions that lie behind female episodes of drama. In the midst of all this, the adolescent female is absorbed with her looks and what peers think of her. Privately, she seems hesitant to relate to something as old fashioned as family values, as her attention is geared toward pleasing peers, texting, and checking statuses on Facebook and other social networks. Who has time for family? Ancient instructions, once clear and defining, are no longer so simple when tied to the unprecedented technological gadgetry she has come to manipulate and refine to meet her needs. Female sapient brains refuse to be unplugged for fear they will miss some random opportunity, usually boy related, so their cell phones stay on all night. (How will these conditions affect the children of today's college students, who are completely immersed in "hot-seconds" communication and turnaround? We simply don't know.)

The overriding question for adolescent females who are quickly sprouting fully equipped young adult bodies is one of superficiality: Am I sexually attractive and desirable enough for a mate? At adolescent puberty, the gentler juvenile years are forever left far behind her as high-gain estrogen, mixed with testosterone, cascades through her brain, making her feel powerful and entitled. She becomes obsessed with her face and body. Being attractive to boys becomes the laser focus of her rapidly developing brain. She's moody, often hardheaded, and completely unpredictable. Puberty has become the defining force in her young life as *gonadatropin-releasing hormone* (GNRH) appears in her hypothalamus and combines with the release of powerful regulating (tropic) hormones from pituitary glands responsible for fertility, such as *follicle-stimulating hormone* (FSH) and *luteinizing hormone* (LH). This chemical tsunami is at the fountainhead of her teenage angst, eroticism, and sexual adventure. It triggers estrogen-progesterone chemical cascades in the hypothalamic-pituitary-ovarian system, engineering changes in her menstrual cycle—the continuous tide of chemistry that defines her moods, both sexual and otherwise, from now until the beginning of perimenopause in her fifties.

Driven by her churning chemistry, her expanded centers for effortless communication, and her need for connection, and exacerbated by her physical-sexual coming of age, it is no wonder that relationship conflicts completely stress her out. The result? She becomes the stereotypical drama queen. Female brain conditions are modulated to respond to relationship conflicts (boyfriend troubles) with nurturance and understanding for his otherwise treacherous behavior, even though her extensive social network of female and male friends don't often agree with her allegiance. Practically on a weekly basis, the ebb and flow of estrogen in her menstrual cycle can produce the all-too-frequent consequences of inconsistent and edgy behavior. "The first two weeks of the cycle, when estrogen is high, a girl is more likely to be socially interested and relaxed with others," Brizendine (2006, 35) notes. "In the last two weeks of the cycle, when progesterone is high and estrogen is low, she is more likely to react with increased irritability and will want to be left alone. Estrogen and progesterone reset the brain's stress response each month. A girl's self-confidence may be high one week but on thin ice the next."

Female flirting is triggered by cascading estrogen and oxytocin, transforming girls' bathrooms in every high school in the world into places to congregate for female bonding. Females love to trade secrets and gossip with girlfriends, a practice that is therapeutic in the game of romance, an antidote to stress and frustration. Dopamine and oxytocin rushes pay huge dividends, brightening moods and nurturing possibilities. With her support group of girlfriends, the adolescent female also forms "game plans" to strategically use against rivals by exposing their deceptive practices while continuing to hide her own varieties. In this process, she hopes to relieve some of her own stress while adding more to her rivals.

Brizendine (2006, 59–60) states, "As Darwin noted, males of all species are made for wooing females, and females typically choose among their suitors. . . . The lessons that early men and women learned are deeply encoded in our modern brains as neurological love circuits."

MALE ADOLESCENT BRAIN CONDITIONS

In contrast, the adolescent male brain, absent chemical tide pools deep into mood regulation and cascading monthly cycles, simply releases a steady and unrelenting cascade of testosterone. The result? He has sexual thoughts every 20 seconds or so during adolescence and part of young adulthood—if you believe reports from pop-culture psychologists. With sex on his brain (sexual focusing and refocusing being the unspoken connection between all adolescent brains), he requires no further need for stimulation or drama. Instead, his brain dictates stereotypical ancient scripts for male posturing, posing, and strutting, with his chest thrust forward above rock hard abdominals, a condition he relishes. Instinctively he is narcissistic, and by that alone he knows he is irresistible to females. According to David Buss of the University of Texas at Austin, men worldwide "prefer physically attractive wives, between ages twenty and forty, who are an average of two and a half years younger than they are. They seek long-term mates who have clear skin, bright eyes, full lips, shiny hair, and curvy, hourglass figures." Most modern sapient-brained species have no idea how important ancient ancestry is in hardwiring into their brains what they find attractive and sexually stimulating in a mate.

Male brains seeking self-advantage every step of the way are more attractive, or appear to be slightly dangerous, and turn out to be the charmers who are sexually attractive to the female brain. Female brains are inherently attracted to handsome and charming narcissists with a gift of gab. He is likely self-absorbed, sporting a bulletproof sense of entitlement, and is already deep into deceptive practices. He employs a variety of dirty tricks to woo multiple females for control and manipulation, even though he swears he's "flying solo." Charming males exhibit the underlying chemistry of brain conditions that articulate into moderate gradations of adaptation and possibly psychopathic maladaptation.

It has already been established by neuroscience that female brains are highly vulnerable to charmers who romance them into intimate relationships. That she bonds too quickly is due to her ubiquitous supply of oxytocin, in evidence when being sexually stimulated and romantically tantalized. In fact, a simple touch, or a whiff of his special cologne or natural pheromones, will stimulate her nurturing and bonding brain.

"I CAN LOVE HIM ENOUGH TO CHANGE HIM"

It's probably true that every female has her own story about attraction and the consequences of falling for Mr. Very Wrong (who at first appeared to be Mr. Right). Reading my students' bios, I discovered females who believed with all their hearts they could change such men; and in most cases, years later and after all the trouble, they still secretly harbored sexual attractions to their wrong choices. Perhaps by age 30 or so, most finally realized what they were up against, but tragically, some never did or ever will. Though it sounds crazy to the uninitiated, examples are everywhere. That's the powerful hold of the charming male, characterized by varieties of corruptors and violent predators. How close are corruptive versions to the violent and pathological version? Too close. Honest individuals mired in worry and concern for others are an easy mark for being set up or blindsided by the crafty and manipulative men who seek self-advantage over others they secretly believe are beneath them.

Generally, the female is, by nature, more nurturing, communicative, verbal, and emotional. She ultimately thrives by being connected to others—her friends, family, and social networks—not by virtue of cognitive appraisal, but by how she feels about them and, ultimately, if she trusts them. Partner-wise, she is out to find Mr. Right and hang onto him, even if she's wrong. She becomes defiant about her choices until she is finally able to see the error of her ways and grows into the realization that her choice was wrong. Yet through it all, she brings a softness to the rough-and-tumble world of males, who seek territory, power, and respect, often by overly aggressive means. As mothers, females bring gentleness, warmth, and love to their families by creating the psychological construct of "home." They nurture progeny before birth and for years after. In most cases, no one can take the place of "mom."

WHAT MEN KNOW BUT DON'T KNOW THEY KNOW

Can lust boost a man's artistic endeavors? Can an attractive female affect a male's creativity? In a documentary called *The Science of Lust* (2011), Professor Vladas Griskevicius of the University of Minnesota states that when an attractive and engaging female—a muse—was inserted into a room where males waited for an assignment to create artwork, sure enough, what they produced in the presence of the muse was judged to be more creative than what they created when they waited by themselves. It was far more stimulating (and creative) to hang out with the muse than to sit alone waiting to be summoned by the professor. Even though the men physically left the room to complete their artistic assignment, mentally the muse was still in their thoughts—a testament to the multifaceted influence of lust, not just for flirting and sex but to boost creativity. The art professor who judged the artwork used the word *agitated* to define the artwork submitted by the males influenced by the muse.

FEMALES GAUGE LUST DIFFERENTLY

Female subjects watched a short promotional video related to tourism versus a video featuring explicit sex. They were asked to rate the experiences of the promo film versus the pornographic film for lustful feelings by indicating responses ranging from 0 to 10 on a handheld monitor. At the same time, the female's heart rate, body temperature, and blood flow to her vagina were being monitored in order to compare them to her visual perceptions. Interesting conclusion: Her physiological responses indicated she was sexually aroused by the sexual video but that her mind was not having any of it: She indicated low arousal to the highly erotic images of the porno film. Most females who watch the pornographic films show similar results. Even though their bodies are engaged in lust, their minds are on cruise control. When men become the subjects, their mental perception is highly correlated to bodily responses of lustful anticipation. Male's brains are "wired" for lust—their brains and bodies are in perfect harmony. Why are men and women mostly different in this regard? What might account for this in evolutionary implications?

According to MRIs, in males, the first brain region to react to sexy images is the amygdala, progressing onward and upward to the ventral striatum, where molecules of dopamine—the chemistry of pleasure—are released in abundance. The final stop is the medial frontal cortex—the CEO of the brain, determining what's next: "down boy" or "get some."

Twenty-four miles per hour is the average speed of cars driven by males on a side street detected by radar guns. When a young and attractive female starts to "strut her stuff" in high heels and a short dress, what changes are likely in the male drivers? The speed of the cars drops to 17 miles an hour and remains there for almost three seconds as the amygdala floods dopamine until, quick as a flash, PFC triggers a momentary pause to "gobble up" the scene before acceleration.

Lust (or romantic desire) on a female's mind influences her to be more cooperative and "nice" to others. Griskevicius assembled a bogus casting call of attractive hopefuls. The first group of women were asked to sit alone until they were called for the interview. The second group shared the room with a couple of handsome, charming, and flirty males. Hidden cameras caught the females being nice to others afterward by helping women gather boxes they had dropped while carrying them to their cars. The women were nice and helpful after talking with the handsome and charming guys. It appears as though you can depend on the kindness of strangers if they have lust on their minds. The group not exposed to males walked right by as though ignoring the women dropping the boxes. Would a nicer female be less likely to cheat on her man later in the relationship? Might she be a better, caring mother in the eyes of males?

The spectrum of lust seems to invade everything we do—if we're feeling lustful. Youth and young adulthood provide the best opportunities for being rewarded by lustful feelings. When men are more lustful, they spend more money and are more attentive to the females they are courting; they also are more sexually aggressive. On the other hand, women are generous sexually and are more altruistic. But, alas, age has a way of muting lust, and the once-plentiful opportunities for expression dry up and "wrinkle" with old age.

MAKING THE CASE FOR THE DIFFERENTLY-ABLED I: ELENA DELLE DONNE (1989–)

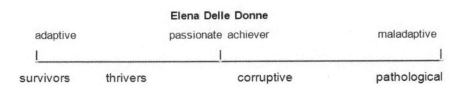

When eight-year-old Elena Delle Donne was in the second grade, her parents hired a personal trainer with the goal of developing their daughter into the new face of American basketball. By eighth grade, she was on the varsity team and was dominating opponents, leaving coaches with no strategies to contain her prodigious abilities. She led her high school team in every category and won all of the postseason awards.

In 2008, Delle Donne was the number-one recruit in America. Obviously, she was destined to land a spot on one of America's best university teams. But which one would win the Delle Donne sweepstakes? Courting a six-foot-five-inch high school junior with guard skills, college coaches from across the nation made their final appeals. When Geno Auriemma, head coach of the perennial winner and national champion University of Connecticut Huskies came calling, Delle Donne answered. Soon she was signed, sealed, and delivered to campus.

But after only two days on the Huskies' court, Delle Donne left campus in the middle of the night. A dumbfounded Coach Auriemma was in shock. "What?" he said. "How? She has no car" (*Connecticut Post,* August 8, 2008). But she was gone, and for good. On reflection, Auriemma had seen the answer for her departure in his prize recruit's eyes: She was homesick. The passion for the game had left her. But homesick for what? Her parents? Her friends? A boyfriend? None of the aforementioned proved to be the answer. Upon hearing the story, former University of Connecticut All-American Kara Wolters said, "It's the most bizarre thing I have ever heard. Better now than to have her affect the team negatively and be like a cancer to the team because she's wacked" (ibid.).

Delle Donne quit the sport she had played with passion for so long, instead playing volleyball as a middle blocker for the University of Delaware. Remarkably, in 2009, she returned to basketball as a member of the Delaware Blue Hens—a team that had never been rated in the top ten. Head Coach Tina Martin saw Delle Donne transform Delaware into the number-eight team in the nation for the first time in history. After three years at Delaware, Delle Donne came full circle from her days at Connecticut, Martin believes. It wasn't that Delle Donne left the game; the problem was what she had left behind at home. Although she missed out on several national championships at Connecticut, that never mattered. Her strength was not on the court, but on the sidelines. Delle Donne missed someone at home who had never seen her play and never will— her older sister, Lizzie.

Elizabeth "Lizzie" Delle Donne was born deaf and blind and stricken with cerebral palsy and autism. She had undergone over 30 surgeries by the time Elena was in her senior year at Delaware. In Elena's words, she and Lizzie have "an unspoken love," and she refers to Lizzie as her "angel" (*Long Island Newsday,* January 23, 2010). During those two days in Connecticut, Elena had lost her connection to her sister. She had to go home.

Elena is able to connect with Lizzie during games by touching her side, where a tattoo of Lizzie's name is surrounded by angel wings. She knows Lizzie gives her strength. If Lizzie can get through what she has to encounter every day, Elena reasons, what's one basketball game? After all, Elena says, "we're family and I have the same DNA she has. Plus," she concludes, "life is way more than a game" (*Long Island Newsday*, January 23, 2010). Elena Delle Donne is our best example of a differently-abled athlete.

MAKING THE CASE FOR THE DIFFERENTLY-ABLED II: LANCE ARMSTRONG (1971–)

		Lance Armstrong	
adaptive		**Corruptive**	maladaptive
I_____	_____	__I_____	_____I
survivors	thrivers	passionate	pathological
		achievers	

Born Lance Edward Gunderson, Lance Armstrong grew up to become a world champion road-racing cyclist. An October 2012 U.S. Anti-Doping Agency report targeted Armstrong with allegations of doping and a cover-up. The report documented sources who testified that Armstrong engineered a scheme that encouraged teammates to dope even as he won the Tour de France a record seven times (1999–2005). Soon after, Armstrong was stripped of his Tour titles (*Encyclopedia Britannica,* 15th ed., s.v. "Lance Armstrong").

On October 17, 2012, Nike, Anheuser-Busch, and other sponsors severed ties with Armstrong due to his participation in doping and his lying to the public about his involvement for more than a decade. On January 17, 2013, he appeared on the Oprah Winfrey Network (OWN) to tell the nation "the truth":

Oprah Winfrey (W):   At the time [of his doping] it did not feel wrong?
Lance Armstrong (A): No. [Pause.] Scary.
W: Did you feel bad about it?
A: No. Even Scarier.
W: Did you feel in any way you were cheating?
A: No. [Pause.] Scariest.

Rather than cheating, Armstrong felt that by doping he was playing on a "level playing field." Through the entire first part of the interview, he did not appear pained or contrite. There were no tears and few laughs. The interview started with simple yes and no answers:

> W: Did you take banned substances?
> A: Yes.
> W: Was one of those EPO?
> A: Yes.
> W: Did you do "blood doping" and use transfusions?
> A: Yes.
> W: Did you use testosterone, cortisone, and HGH [human growth hormone]?
> A: Yes.
> W: Did you take banned substances or blood dope in all of your tour wins?
> A: Yes.

During and after the Tour de France wins, Armstrong vehemently denied doping and quickly cast aside teammates who suggested otherwise. He swore he raced clean. His relentless pursuit of "settling any score on his terms" is what he regretted the most—"that's inexcusable," he concluded.

The fallout from sponsors was like a dam bursting. In a statement, Nike said, "We do not condone the use of illegal performance enhancing drugs in any manner. . . . We have been duped by his denials over the years" (*Los Angeles Times,* January 18, 2013). Minutes after Nike's blistering statement, Armstrong announced he was stepping down as the chairman of his beloved cancer-fighting charity, Livestrong.

PART III

Giving It a Go with a Psycho

Chapter 9

Je ne Sais Quoi

READERS' PRE-TEST

Sometimes, a person has qualities of behavior and mannerisms that cannot be put into words. True or false?

The answer is true.

A youthful adolescent does not see the same world as a mature, adult person. True or False?

The answer is true.

You only live once, but it helps if you get to be young twice.

Matthew (Michael Caine) in *Blame It on Rio* (1984)

JE NE SAIS QUOI: THERE'S JUST SOMETHING ABOUT YOU

Alpha males and alpha females often possess strong sexual "messages" that cannot be put into words. One would be hard pressed to find a more engaging expression than the French phrase *Je ne sais quoi*—which literally means "I don't know what" and describes an individual's almost magical qualities—charm, sex appeal, and demeanor that are hard to put into words. The expression fits the alphas of our species—male and female "leaders and breeders" who are society's "movers and shakers," possessing the ambition and drive characteristic of moderate variations of excitatory chemistry. The "moderates"—the ones who possess drive, ambition, and focus—often comprise society's innovators and top-flight achievers. Usually, they get what they seek . . . eventually. Maybe they possess "dangerous qualities" similar to "bad boys," while female varieties are often statuesque and gorgeous, the ones who are often asked, "Aren't you a model?" Still, both male and female varieties are noticed immediately—they light up a room with their allure. Clearly, they have more options than most. From perfect bodies to beautiful smiles, smarts, and animal magnetism—what do they have? They have a certain *je ne sais quoi.*

North American culture features beehives of glamorous people from pop culture—individuals who possess celebrity, good looks, money, and charm—the ones most often observed in celebrity-focused shows. In fact, the most popular American TV programs in prime time are competition shows featuring singers, dancers, survivors, biggest losers, and would-be chefs. Then there's the obsession with "relationship dramas," always top choices, and "crime dramas." With this constant saturation in mind, we now turn to the evolution of charm and its power for "Prince Charming" alpha males, and the head-to-head competition sure to unfold when the beautiful and talented meet other differently-abled competitors and those less proficient in the games of sex, mating, and making one's own way in the world. We must address the significance of the spectrum with accompanying stengths (high levels) and weaknesses (low levels), and rationale for maladaptation to reach valid conclusions, such as:

Both extremely high and extremely low levels of psychopathy may be maladaptive, with *intermediate levels being most adaptive.* The basis for saying that high levels of psychopathy are maladaptive is, of course, the trouble into which clinical psychopaths often get themselves. The basis for saying that low levels of psychopathy may also be maladaptive stems from the common role of anxiety in psychopathy: psychopaths do not seem to show any anxiety [emphasis added]. (Dutton 2012, 123)

THE ALPHAS

Alphas tend to pursue each other and, when united, make "power couples." For such couples to be productive and nurturing, they must respect each other, somewhat of a rarity in behavior for alphas, who tend to be narcissistic to a degree often bordering on arrogance. But in cases in which alpha couples are respectful and nurturing of the relationship, the pairing can produce staggering successes. A prime example is the union of Helen Gurley Brown and David Brown, two examples of alphas who possess considerable social skills and "smarts."

Putting *je ne sais quoi* into the formula for alphas, we now address how exploitative and predatory they can be. Non-alpha females who "buy" everything "dished out" by alpha males usually get swatted like flies in the end. However, because of her "special weapons and tactics" (physical gifts from nature and remarkable intuition), the alpha female is ahead of the curve, as Helen Gurley proved to be, in landing her choice of a mate. Yet simply as a passing fancy or for sexual thrills, alpha females may exploit guys as sexual "boy toys."

It is frustrating to many, especially the average female's parents, when she selects Mr. Very Wrong (a.k.a. the "bad boy"). Mr. Very Wrong feels perfectly entitled to exploit and deceive her as his manipulated prey. He celebrates being "God's gift" as women "melt" at his charming touch. Over the course of a 27-year study of adolescent brains and behavior, I have asked students to write an autobiographical essay that answers the question "Who Are You and Why? Be Honest in fewer than 10 pages." According to one of my students in her autobiography, "I just can't get by without his touch, his voice and charm. Otherwise, most of the time, he's a *jerk.*"

In an article about the appeal of the "bad boy," Nando Pelusi (2009), states:

In its pernicious version, bad becomes "really bad," as in psychopathy. The psychopath takes advantage of people's implicit trust, and has evolved a strategy that opportunistically seeks out victims. Even when he's not physically dangerous, a compulsively fun-loving rogue, in love with his own social power, can waste a lot of time, notably a woman's reproductive time, with his unwillingness to commit. Females are the choosier sex, and males compete for their attention. The result of the competition is that men have evolved strategies such as seeking alpha status.

Surely our early ancestors, the Cro-Magnons, started the behavior we see today. For example, did curvaceous, green-eyed "Dimple-Cheeks" choose "Alpha Hairy-Legs," who claimed to others he was out hunting caribou with his buddies but was secretly fooling around with his new conquest inside his provocateur's cave? Are modern females still choosing modern bad boys disguised as male charmers? Is the female brain naturally drawn to the magnet of the bad boy's slightly dangerous but charming male?

Is it possible for females to alter their genetic makeup to view deceptive charmers more realistically? For the most part, the answer is a tentative maybe. Even with a fully functional prefrontal cortex, students indicated through many of their bios that females still get "weak in the knees" when these special males look their way. We contend the modern scenario has not changed dramatically from the ancient script. If the male is charming, by implication, being a deceptive chronic liar is easy and effective, practically guaranteeing he can make most females "melt" at the sight of him. Are female sapient brains vulnerable (gullible) from ancient scripts for pair bonding? Judging by more than two thousand student bios and counting, it is a foundational neurotruth that the young females of our species are overwhelmingly vulnerable to the charms of handsome males.

GULLIBILITY

Gullibility is the brain condition of being easily deceived, especially by charm. Even in the face of negative chatter from others, for example, the gullible female tends to continually ignore sound advice from those she should trust, such as her best friends and parents. Often, truthfulness from others is a complete washout when it comes to questioning her choice for Mr. Right. It seems her gullibility, as well as pair bonding to the object of her obsession, are hardwired into her young, developing female brain. Nature's gift of industrial-strength oxytocin, her "glue" for social and pair bonding, is highly effective in "cementing" her choice.

Brain-wise, it is also a neurotruth that *his* brain features predatory agendas. Here's another one for my stable—his intoxicating charms and good looks cover his narcissism, which appears to her as confidence. In her mind she truly feels special and deserving of the undivided attention he lavishes upon her. Parents become mentally and physically exhausted trying to talk their young and naïve teenage daughters out of embracing bad choices in potential mates. In evolutionary terms, the young female has to learn for herself how first impressions can be so misleading; she must advance by trial and error to her final selection—a selection that often retains features of the "man who got away," the man who broke her heart, the man with a certain *je ne sais quoi*. Along the way, she will pick up valuable lessons about evaluating suitable males who will make (hopefully) good husbands and caring fathers.

In one of my classes, one exasperated student—a middle-aged mother with three teenage girls—suggested in class that raising teenagers must have prompted those in antiquity to create the "hell-fire" aspect of religion—the sinners' punishment of eternal damnation in hell's unquenchable fires. Many older females in the class nodded their heads in approval.

In the developing field of evolutionary neuropsychology, here are a few questions to consider relative to mate selection:

- Does it benefit species reproduction for the female brain to be gullible to charmers? Do charmers have good genes?
- Does it benefit the production of progeny if the male brain is relatively predatory—translated into being aggressive and territorial in the mating sweepstakes? Does this behavior suggest some characteristics of psychopathy?
- Does the charm of a corruptive or pathological psychopath disarm evidence of possible harm (hiding his inability to love and to nurture a partner)?
- Does love and tenderness from female mates suppress or mitigate male aggressive tendencies?
- Is charm one of a handful of highly effective "helpful traits" of natural selection driving the continuation of our species?

Nothing, it now seems, is more naturally selected by the engines of evolution than adaptive and moderate versions of the chemistry behind "special weapons and tactics"—behavioral strategies for achieving prominence, wealth, and influence and thus gaining access to attractive mates. Does she nurture his moderate gradations of what the world persists in calling (incorrectly) psychopathy, thereby strengthening the possibility he will be a good provider producing wealth for her and her children? The sexual magnetism of his or her certain *je ne sais quoi* keeps the competition for mates quite interesting.

THE HALO EFFECT AND *JE NE SAIS QUOI*

Over the 27-year history of Professor Jacobs's student bios, indications from adolescents themselves confirm time and again that females appear to possess a distinct vulnerability to being blindsided by charming males. A recurring theme of adolescent females suggests that the Mr. Right in their pasts excelled at spinning cocoons of silky promises, interspersed with lies, around her, cemented by his engaging smile and good looks. She became transfixed and was "putty in his hands." At first, good sex sealed the deal, but that often changed abruptly when he demanded more perverted varieties of sex. How many times have we heard young females say, "I just wanted to please him"?

From neuroscience, we discover the halo effect of male charm, which allows the male to make numerous missteps and misalliances, covering his tracks with compulsive lies. And the female falls hard—"head over heels," according to the popular saying. Truly, love allows females to be blind-sided. In a PET scan, her brain's midbrain limbic system lights up with a flurry of chemical activity in contrast to her dimly lit prefrontal cortices. The "jazzing" chemistry of the MLS makes her increasingly vulnerable to being controlled and manipulated by her charmer. Interestingly, telling lies required more activity in the prefrontal cortex of the frontal lobes than telling the truth.

By contrast, imagine the male brain's bonding chemistry as a watered-down version of females' industrial-strength oxytocin—his version being vasopressin, which doubles as an attack chemical. He is less captured by her female drama while laser-focused on her evolutionarily mandated hor-mone "markers"—her physical sexuality personified by her individualized body parts. By his smile and good looks, and by being shirtless to the waist, nature is on his side, as his torso secretes pheromones that command interested females to look his way.

Being vulnerable to charmers, females can be swept off their feet and fall in love fairly routinely and predictably, a process accomplished largely by the male persuasion of deceptive ruses. Charm stimulates her "lust chemistry," chiefly her PEA brain, which sends cascades of "romantic" chemistry coursing through her brain. The anticipation of physical pleasure and emotional fireworks from her DANE brain is further enhanced by her robust supply of testosterone. By contrast, the male brain basks in the glow of being an aggressive "player," enticing female brains to risk everything for his touch. Often, he employs deception that may be directed toward her or her girlfriends, whom she may start to distrust as competition heats up. The most damaging component of deception is how a charmer can charm the very life out of his prey in violent, pathological versions. In the brain's architectural wiring, gender differences do exist in the mating game as we disclosed in an earlier chapter. But differences exist at the neurotransmitter and hormonal levels by subtle gradation.

To briefly reiterate, cerebral facts and figures discovered down deep in the innermost recesses of sapient brains have emerged in the age of neuro-science. Such neurological facts are expressed in this text as neurotruths, which evolved from cutting-edge information extracted from the flurry of research that produced journal articles and textbooks from the Decade of the Brain (1990–1999) to the present day. There can be no doubt that brain conditions from our excitatory chemistry (DANE and PEA brainmarks and testosterone and oxytocin efficacy enhanced by DHEA) are powerful determinants of behavior. As a result, we are tenacious and resilient from birth, and as we develop in social milieus we possess powerful cognitive-mapping thought patterns that are highly individualistic, eventually triggering maturity of the PFC to produce our species' differently-abled brains. With such power and diversity, who or what can stop us when we feel passion and resolve?

Anyone who cares to notice—our *res ipsa* argument—can see evidence for themselves and similarly observe in others the intoxicating power of lustful chemistry that supercharges our brains. For sure, there's nothing to match the aphrodisiac-like quality inherent in our brains when we encounter the essence of *je ne sais quoi.*

> *I don't know what he had, but whatever it was seemed magical. I became putty in his hands; he shaped me into what I became: a sexual object. At the time, I was sure I could change him into my ideal guy. I would listen to no one . . . but him. I don't know how I came to my senses. One day I just left him; my family and I disappeared into another town. I closed down my social network sites and changed my cell number. Then I struggled for years to regain my sense of self. I continued to look over my shoulder for years when I felt the presence of another behind me. This is going to sound shocking and "way out there" but I am sure he raped or killed someone, somewhere. I was very fortunate to escape his domination. In every way, he had me right where he wanted me and I served myself up to him every time like a satisfying meal. It's all so depressing now to think how much I lost of myself.*

Student autobiographical essay, 2012

SKIN HUNGER

Females are a curious species due to vigorous brain conditions that produce "skin hunger," absent the accustomed touch and caress of her skin. Plentiful *res ipsa* observations show she will stay in a torturous relationship for a combination of reasons, including chemical spikes from contact comfort. This neurologically inspired halo effect of experiences shows the central importance of sexual pair bonding and subsequent memories tied to these experiences. Across the spectrum, she misses everything about him—his charming smile, engaging humor, gentle caresses, and passionate kisses. In some cases, even in abuse, she unfortunately feels that mistreatment is better than being alone.

Her natural internal alarm system (the amygdala), normally responsive to "creepy" feelings as a physiological defense against harm, is disarmed by his charm. Her alarm thus muted, he comes across as neither creepy nor repugnant, although he may appear a bit dangerous, a confounding condition.

In the very beginning of romance, the worst-case scenario is the likelihood that a charming male may be a psychopathic charmer. If this is the case, he has a far right pedigree on our spectrum—a predatory stalker and killer. He is a charming prince typified by a trapdoor spider that lurks beneath his polished veneer, making him real trouble from the first kiss. His gradation of powerful chemistry, reinforced by his cognitive mapping, may put his prey in real emotional jeopardy since corruptive and pathological psychopaths are incapable of three things: love, remaining monogamous (or becoming a loving and caring mate), and becoming a nurturing parent.

The male brain is turbocharged by churning testosterone, which supercharges his sensibilities to target female hormone-markers. All of his male accouterments (the physical gifts of good looks, charm, and washboard abs) enhance his torso-secreting pheromones, intent upon luring an entourage of females, fronted by his "special lady." This scenario reigned supreme in male and female sapient brains prior to the current national obsession of social networking, the rise of the pseudo-celebrity culture, and the "hot seconds" expectations from instant text messaging. One can only imagine what it's going to be like to raise kids who have yet to enter middle school, with all they have available in social networking. We have few if any reliable studies of how electronic gadgetry will influence our human condition long term, but it appears evident the effect will be considerable (though nothing our amazing brains cannot handle).

THE NEW BRAIN

What are modern parents to do when surrounded by the images of pop culture blitzing their progeny's cell phones and electronic tablets? More than likely, it will take both parents to consistently draw lines in the sand and hold their ground, plus the advice of grandparents still living on the planet, the support of younger and older siblings, and a generous helping of dumb luck. Keep in mind that a teenage daughter has no problem with throwing everyone in the family "under the bus" in favor of her latest version of Prince Charming. In this arena of her life, she means business.

Through dangerous developmental stages, young sapient brains consistently answer the bell of titillating escapades into the unknown with an array of maneuvering, deceptive practices fueled by the anticipation of confronting new sources of stimulation. The truth is, adolescent and young adult brains bore easily, especially with all the modern technological gadgetry at hand to manipulate cognition away from the real world and into the virtual one. Thus the dangerous allure of novel adventures may approach an obsession in young brains. Such activities can lead to serious drug experimentation, addiction, and fatal accidents, primarily of the overdose and automotive varieties.

Self-absorbed narcissism and self-righteous entitlement (allowing a self-imposed free reign to do as one pleases regardless of consequence) are often accomplished magnificently by fabrications of truth and cover-ups. It's similar to the well-established psychological dynamics of Festinger's *cognitive-dissonance* paradigm in which lying becomes the best strategy to overcome adolescents' "dissonance" (conflicts) caused by parents saying no. So adolescents get what they want by lying, and parents think they've won. Yet parents have been fed false information from their bright-eyed children for so long that they go to sleep in their warm beds believing one thing while their children are out of their sight doing something else entirely. Very effectively and most convincingly, deception makes everyone happy.

Being a parent myself of four teenagers across four decades, and reading the nearly 20,000 student bios written in the 1970s, 1980s, 1990s, and 2000s, I would say that parents in general know less than 10 percent of what their children are really doing. Adolescent students have boasted about their deceptive practices. Many even boasted of dangerous dirty tricks such as drinking and driving and illegal drug experimentation. In my students' autobiographical essays, I received more than I expected. Most often, I received over 10 pages; my longest response was 60 pages. Did some students lie and stretch the truth in their responses? Of course, but that possibility yields a salient point as well—we expect some deception up front, but kernels of truth do emerge when repeated over 100 semesters. The greatest of those truths is this: Over the years, students from all walks of life have overcome incredible odds—horrendous abuses and bullying, addictions, and nearly losing their lives due to really bad decisions with no substantive morality other than common sense—and remained tenacious (and perhaps lucky) enough to end up, class schedule in hand, as members of my college classrooms. I am convinced, beyond a reasonable doubt, of the reality of adaptive neurochemistry as the most powerful brain condition promoting surviving and thriving and, in the differently-abled, soaring achievements in successful careers.

As Homo sapiens, we sharpen our special weapons and tactics (deception, lying, retaliation, and cover-up) in life's most dangerous stages of development (adolescence) to gain advantages in the often brutal and dramatic competition for relationships and partners. This condition continues in how we care for our progeny, how we launch successful careers in the workplace, and how we buy homes, cars, and the necessities of life. Today, due to rapid advances in digital technologies and social networking, young sapient brains have been tweaked or "rewired" over the version of sapient brains from just 15 years ago. In the current age of the neuroscience, high-definition brain neuroscans have given scientists and forensic investigative neuroscientists the ability to observe blood flow activity in live brains. The interconnected pathways delivering powerful chemistry to deep cortical regions and receptors can now be mapped, allowing us to see the process that furnishes the "power and light" to our diverse adaptive "toolboxes," the chemically driven weapons and tactics developed through the dynamics of natural selection. Such maneuvering is required in human venues as the perpetual spotlight focuses upon competition for mates and resources. We had better be tenacious and resilient if we want to get our share at the banquet table.

As testimony to the power and deceptive practices inherent in our sapient brains, what we truly want we usually get one way or the other. In the pathological gradation of spectrum psychopathy, violent and sexualized dirty tricks run the gambit, producing horrific crime scenes that ironically make those responsible into media celebrities. While this may at first seem shocking, the dark side of our wondrous brains are becoming known in the age of neuroscience.

MAKING THE CASE FOR THE DIFFERENTLY-ABLED I: JENNIFER BRICKER (1987–)

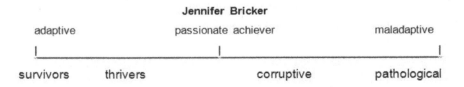

A young girl born without legs and abandoned at the hospital when her parents discovered her massive disability, Jennifer Bricker grew up in an adoptive family. The Brickers had three sons of their own when they decided it wasn't right for anyone to abandon a legless baby in a hospital.

As Jennifer grew into young childhood, she came to love watching the sport of gymnastics on TV. Her adoptive parents told Jennifer that *can't* was the only word she could never use. So her parents allowed Jennifer to take gymnastic lessons, to the amazement of onlookers who marveled at her extraordinary abilities. At the time, there were no competitions such as the Paralympic Games for athletes with disabilities, so being differently-abled, she was allowed to compete with normally-abled gymnasts.

The reason for Jennifer's gymnastics obsession was a 14-year-old Romanian gymnast by the name of Dominique Moceanu, who dazzled the world by being part of the American team winning the gold medal as part of the "Magnificent Seven"—seven team members competing in the 1996 Olympic Games in Atlanta, Georgia. In her floor exercise, Dominique performed a nearly flawless routine to the music of "The Devil Came Down to Georgia."

Remarkably, Jennifer Bricker would eventually become a decorated gymnast upon graduation from high school. As she grew older, she would soon meet her famous sister, Dominique. Yes, they had been sisters all along. It had been Dominique's parents who had abandoned Jennifer at the hospital. The two had a lot to talk about, and they were quickly embraced by Dominique's other sister, Christina.

MAKING THE CASE FOR THE DIFFERENTLY-ABLED II: DICK FOSBURY (1947–)

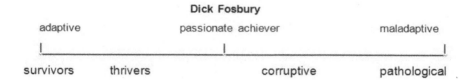

Richard Douglas "Dick" Fosbury revolutionized the popular field event of high jumping by creating a new technique: flying over the bar backward in what would eventually be called the "Fosbury flop." By age 16, Fosbury started experimenting with his "back-over-first" innovation, which was in stark contrast to the traditional "straddle" and the then nearly obsolete "scissors" method. The straddle method involved "rolling" over the bar face down after a mighty leap, lifting each leg sequentially over the bar, while the older scissors method featured running toward the bar and leaping over with upper body ramrod straight as each leg scissored over the bar. Neither technique worked for Fosbury (*Encyclopedia Britannica*, 15th ed., s.v. "Dick Fosbury").

As a junior at Medford High School in Oregon, he broke the school record with a jump of six feet and three inches. Coaches stopped criticizing his new technique after he experienced success. By his senior year in high school he had, by trial and error, refined his new method by curving his body—back first—over the bar and kicking both legs up in the air at the end of the jump. He captured second place in the state meet with a jump of six feet and five and a half inches. As he steadily cleared higher bars, media coverage exploded around the world. Yet many jumpers poked fun at Fosbury's "flop," at first thinking he looked like the laziest higher jumper in the world. Yet Fosbury remained committed and refined his methods in college at Oregon State University. In 1968, he won the NCAA title and gained a place on the U.S. Olympic team headed for Mexico City.

One last problem had to be resolved for the flop. It became evident that the landing exposed the jumper's head and shoulder to injury, as jumpers landed backward, with seven feet or more to drop, into sawdust or sand. And then, almost overnight, seemingly as a gesture to accommodate Fosbury's innovation, softer material for the landing pit, such as foam rubber held together in mesh nets, appeared and became the standard. This was soon followed by entire landing pits on wheels made of a "block" of soft, synthesized rubber encased in weather-resistant covering. Better still, the new "pit" was elevated three feet above ground level, which was perfect for a backward landing.

At the 1968 Mexico City games, Fosbury captured the gold medal and a new Olympic record of 7 feet and 4.25 inches (2.24 meters). The Fosbury flop had made it all the way to the Olympics and won. It is now the standard for all high jumpers, male and female, around the world. Today, Fosbury is a member of Champions for Peace, a group of 54 elite athletes committed to peace in the world through sports. He and follow Olympians Gary Hall Sr. and Anne Cribbs are also founders of World Fit, a nonprofit organization promoting youth fitness programs and Olympic ideals (*Encyclopedia Britannica,* 15th ed., s.v. "Dick Fosbury").

Chapter 10

Evolution of the Prefrontal Cortex

READERS' PRE-TEST

The prefrontal cortex matures as we develop through childhood discoveries, the drama of adolescence, and into young adulthood. It might be age 30 before it fully develops, practically guaranteeing that individuals will make more responsible choices based upon consequences as they age. True or False?

The answer is true.

> *The mind is its own place, and it itself can make a Heaven of Hell, a Hell of Heaven.*

John Milton

> *Talent does what it can; genius does what it must.*

Edward Bulwer-Lytton

Adapting to troubles by finding solutions is as much of a neurotruth today as it was in ancient times. Survival scripts arm sapient brains with headstrong chemistry for "strong backbones," "tough skins," and "feisty gumption." The chemistry of strong willpower comes "factory sealed" in sapient brains, sharpened or dulled by life's experiences.

Nature has gifted us with chemical inoculations against our usual torrential downpour of problems, frustrations, depressions, and heartbreaking experiences.

> It is currently coming to light that within the frontal lobes, the prefrontal dorsolateral cortex is the center charged with making plans that the orbitofrontal cortex decides to carry out or not. The ventromedial cortex, for its part, assigns emotional meaning to our perceptions and actions. A dysfunctional ventromedial cortex would, then, cause emotions not to be assigned to actions or to be assigned incorrectly.
>
> (Raine and Sanmartin 2001)

PREFRONTAL CORTEX: THE SAVIOR OF SAPIENT BRAINS

Prefrontal cortices within the frontal lobes of sapient brains—left-side and right-side portions, near mirror images of each other—can be characterized as the epicenter of *cognitive reconsideration,* leading eventually to going forward with plans, suspending action by reconsidering alternatives, or stopping cold and abandoning plans altogether.

Within the frontal lobes, making plans, problem solving, and brainstorming are specifically assigned to the dorsolateral PFC. This component probes past experiences for relevance of possible outcomes in present and future choices. In close proximity, the ventromedial PFC is marked by chemistry firing up emotional feedback, adding a dash of personal feelings to the problem under consideration. It remains for the orbitofrontal PFC—the dashboard of the brain, located right behind our foreheads and just above our eyes—to provide selective attention and the cognitive process of deciding (or not) to move forward, wait and decide later, or suspend or abandon plans.

It is evolutionarily mandated that this region—the OFPFC—is the final tollbooth of cognitive reconsideration and realization of consequence; it is the benchmark of sapient-brained species, defining the very essence of the word *sapient.* That is, as a self-aware species, we factor in experiences and realize that consequences are very real and potentially long-lasting. This condition marks the central difference between adolescent developmental brains, mature and responsible adults, and corruptive and pathological psychopaths—who have consistently shown frontal lobe abnormalities.

PFC aspects of the frontal lobes are configured from ancient survival scripts comprising a mix of chemistry to initiate intellect, feelings, reasoning, and memory in the shaping and maintaining of affect, cognition, and behavior. Often the PFC dampens impulses from the midbrain limbic system, the region awash in the DANE brain adolescent stage of knee-jerk impulsivity, leaping into immediate gratification before the all-important scan of cognitive reconsideration. As the PFC develops from the intellectual rigors of academic training and the physical and psychological maturity of accumulated experiences, adolescent brains transition into a brain of "second thoughts," a brain of "looking before leaping" in the mid- to late 20s and sometimes as late as the early 30s. The growth toward cognitive reconsideration continues into the late 50s and even early 60s, when people become "worry warts," overthinkers, and over-analyzers.

It is not stretching the point to suggest the PFC is the savior of sapient brains. Why? Because brainstorming, problem solving, cognitive reconsideration, and second thoughts have moved our species to the top of the food chain. We make far fewer fatal mistakes by this process. Also, we have an abundance of excitatory chemistry to get what we want if we can just figure out what our true passions are, a chore often accomplished by one's early 20s. In the maturing PFC, so-called higher-order activities such as restraint, creativity, strategy, inspiration, and hesitation allow second thoughts to predominate behavior, and this is, above all, the mark of attaining adulthood. With maturity of the PFC, parents can finally take a deep sigh of relief. Many young adults look back on how difficult it must have been for their parents to have raised them to maturity in light of their know-it-all attitude, impulsivity, and hardheadedness. Later these young adults often find the courage to finally admit, "I get it! I was just stupid at that age and wouldn't listen to anybody. Now I see my payback will be well deserved when I have to raise my own teenagers."

As movement is required for physical action, regions in the posterior aspects of the frontal lobes—the *premotor cortex* and *motor cortex*—trigger, modify, or stop movement as dictated by chemical instruction from the OFPFC. Areas in close proximity to frontal lobes as well as the *neocortex,* which covers the top of the cerebrum like an ultra-thin cap, display how the brain's functionality musters strength and power from multidisciplinary and interdisciplinary connectivity. The powerful chemistry behind tenacity, resilience, bulletproof feelings of invincibility, and passion practically guarantees survival. It's no different with psychopaths—they possess the same vigorous brain conditions—with major differences: perversity, arrogance, and violence leading to destruction and social disharmony. They don't see the same world as do the rest of us.

OUR "STACKED BRAIN"

Located at the top of the brain just behind the frontal lobes, the *parietal lobes* contain the *sensory cortexes,* characterized by sensation (touch and pressure) and an association area for refining sensation. The *temporal lobes,* one lobe on each side of the brain at the level of the ears, help detect sounds and smells, sorting new information in rapid-fire succession, with possible implications for short-term memory. The right lobe is involved in visual memory, while the left lobe processes verbal memory. Finally, the *occipital lobe,* located in the most caudal (back) aspect of the brain, is involved in processing visual information and houses association areas for visual modification.

The middle regions of the brain, comprised of the midbrain and limbic systems, blaze with colors in neuroscans, indicating substantial blood flow as glucose is metabolized in the form of the powerful reward chemistry of the DANE brainmark. At puberty, the tsunami of chemical influences leading to sexual development converges in the MLS, where such powerful chemistry often acts as a "bully" to poorly performing, traumatized, or immature PFC regions—resulting in the behavioral impulsivity and lack of second thoughts often observed in adolescence. It is *res ipsa* evident that the developmental stage of adolescence provides the breezeway into addiction and juvenile crime. Parents must draw deep lines into the shifting sands of adolescent sensibilities, creating clear consequences until their children develop their prefrontal cortices because it only gets worse with pathological psychopathy and the willingness to take lives.

The bottommost regions of the brain define territoriality and obsessive-compulsive behavior, as the brain stem functions with designs on emotion, learning, sexuality, and memory, connecting upward to the midbrain and the limbic system and extending connections all the way to the neocortex and prefrontal regions.

DEEP DOWN IN THE BRAIN OF MONSTERS

In *Whoever Fights Monsters* (1992) and *Mind Hunter* (1995), former FBI agents Robert Ressler and John Douglas, respectively, describe the violence of serial killers who operate as though driven by animalistic instincts rather than the human qualities normally expressed in sapient brains by the evolution of the PFC. By utilizing the bottom two-thirds of their brains as driving forces of behavior, somehow their arrogance and grandiose arrogance fueled corruptive and pathological psychopathy. Neurologically, it is not a big leap in logic to suggest the architecture of our "stacked" brain is more than meta-phorical, as lower regions reflect ancient centers capable of brutality and rapacious behavior—stalking and attacking live prey with on-the-fly preda-tory violence.

Violent sexual predators most often operate from the bottom and mid-dle of the cerebral "deck," where chemical cascades of DANE, PEA, and testosterone provide powerful sexualized brainmarks of impulsivity that seek instant gratification. As such, weakly performing, traumatized, or un-derdeveloped PFC regions become overwhelmed and cannot handle the overload. Operating in the higher PFC regions, forensic investigative sci-entists realize from their training that those operating in the lower centers of the MLS and brain stem—predators who are obsessive and compulsive—will eventually display impulsivity, resulting in serious mistakes.

As mentioned earlier, the PFC, as the dashboard of the brain, is lo-cated directly behind the forehead. Here, various meninges add layer upon layer of protection to insulate delicate cerebral tissue, which has a natural consistency of chilled Jell-O. It was the OFPFC region, in the landmark study of murderers by the University of Southern California's Adrian Raine and others, that showed damage in violent murderers, rap-ists, and serial killers. When subjects are asked to perform mental exer-cises known to fire up the PFC, such activity is normally indicated by bright colors (reds and yellows), indicative of healthy blood flow and an active metabolism. Instead, the scans of violent offenders appeared "cool coded" (shades of light blue), indicative of a low metabolism and/or low blood flow. Clearly, in these cases the OFPFC was disabled and incapaci-tated. Without a fully functioning PFC, impulses cannot be dampened or blocked from ancient regions supercharged with impulsivity, emotion, sexuality, and violent impulses of aggression. Thus the offenders' vio-lent urges rose from deep within the brain and, unmitigated by a defunct PFC, passed from impulse into action.

Furthermore, according to neurologist Antonio Damasio (1994), dam-age to the ventromedial sector can be equally as problematic by profoundly disrupting social behavior. In patients who were previously well adapted, injury to this region translated into an inability to observe social conven-tions and make mature decisions. Remarkably, patients' intellectual abili-ties were generally unaffected in the sense that they continued to have normal learning, memory, language, and attention as reflected in executive function tests such as the Wisconsin Card Sorting Test. However, these same individuals displayed abnormality in processing emotions to the ex-tent that they did not experience normal emotions in relation to complex situations and events. For example, the "emotion and ensuing feeling of embarrassment . . . induced by specific social contexts" was no longer observed (Damasio 1994). Damasio's study, though not directly conducted on violent psychopathic offenders, holds striking implications. When paired with the maladaptive functions of restraint in the PFC, malfunctions in the VMPFC could produce the ability to display expected social behaviors without experiencing the normally attached emotion. Thus victims are drawn into a carefully modeled ruse by someone who feels none of the required emotional attachment to human life or remorse for taking it.

ARE WE A DEAD SPECIES WALKING?

Today, pop culture seems to give top billing to general audiences seeking the mindless drama and gibberish of celebrities, so that discovering truths relative to our human condition is summarily ignored and placed on the back burner. Americans in general, for reasons largely unknown, seem disconnected from embracing science. Yet in the age of neuroscience, it appears increasingly warranted that parents, educators, and anyone seeking better lives must reset their courses to embrace the facts about our brains uncovered through great strides in research over the past 20 years.

Possessing willpower and hope, the gifts of nature's cascading chemistry, keeps us acutely aware of using our heads as we navigate the rough spots of life, which we now encounter with the added stress of living in a world in which communication and feedback can occur in a matter of seconds. We contend the result has steadily eroded away the patience required for waiting. Instant text messaging is not called "instant" for nothing. Added to that, the unprecedented social networking of the Internet and this technological gadgetry has revolutionized response times. The terms *friend* and *fan* have taken on entirely new meanings. Has this condition produced a dangerous and deadly trend as we become rapidly included in others' lives? Shouldn't we know more about "friends" than what is shared online? Is it too outrageous to suggest we may be a dead species walking? We think not.

As this book constantly affirms, our amazing brain is fully capable of handling life's currently accelerated pace and any new wrinkles thrown our way by the advance of technology. So Generation X cohorts (individuals whose birthdates range from the mid-1960s to 1980s) and Generation Y cohorts (with birthdates from the 1990s to 2000) may have lost patience or are destined to lose patience. Though the older generation (baby boomers, with birthdates from 1946 to 1964) may deplore all of what teenagers and young adults have grown accustomed to, history has shown that life goes on as our remarkable brains are marvels of adaptation. Today, the increased connectivity is nothing our brains can't handle.

One of the crowning achievements and value of education is (and has always been) to kick-start the intellectual process of PFC development. For those who have never considered the profound importance of this contribution, it is time.

FROM THE BEAT GENERATION TO THE CHEAT GENERATION

In America, the 1950s was characterized by an adolescent "underground" youth movement—beatniks—espousing sexual shenanigans, alcohol consumption, and drug experimentation. Beatniks were the precursors to hippies—the youth movement of the late 1960s and early 1970s, which on the surface embraced love and peace but also attacked middle-class values and launched the sexual revolution of the 1960s and 1970s. Youth movements often mask the darker side of the use of drugs such as LSD ("acid") and marijuana ("reefer"),

Today, the electronic stylus of cell phones and Internet social networking have yet again reconfigured the modern adolescent brain. Self-absorbed narcissism embodied by self-marketing has never been more prolific in America. Could it be that adaptive versions of the neurospectrum have moved further to the right on the spectrum, meaning increased narcissism and self-indulgent entitlement? And would this be a good or bad condition? Have adaptive varieties of surviving been ratcheted up into the pressure to achieve beyond what is capable from young and developing brains? Said another way, have the youth of America become pressured to achieve and win in everything they attempt? Could this "push becoming a shove" result in achieving at any price—even to the extent of becoming corruptive? Or have others, powerless to achieve such outlandishly high expectations, become resigned to complacency?

It seems untenable to suggest that the combined influences of social revolutions prominent in the 1960s, the "me generation" of the 1970s and 1980s, and the ongoing greed and financial scandals and rise of pseudo-celebrity obsession in the 2000s have not contributed in profound ways to moving brain conditions toward grandiose narcissism and bulletproof entitlement for some and feelings of being overwhelmed with higher expectations for others. It really comes down to how individuals are differently abled by biology and how social influences contribute to or inhibit progress toward self-realization. Still, it appears the vast majority of American citizens continue to be glued to the TV, watching the lullabies of reality shows and juicy yet meaningless drivel from late night shows. Meanwhile, today's youth forge ahead with increasing entitlement, glued to computer screens in gluttonous social networking sessions without a thought of consequences. No predictable filters exist on either side for those who only appear to be who they pretend to be.

It is our argument that sapient brain "wiring" and "rewiring," beginning with nature's adaptive gradations, are stronger today than in the decade of the 1960s, a time just prior to the all-encompassing influences of most modern technology. But arguments pro and con to our position will continue to evolve. As long as profits and demand drive the newest editions of gadgetry, the obsession for "connection" will continue to soar.

OBLIVION OF PATIENCE

In the space of a decade, cutting-edge software technologies have affected young brains toward a bloated self-absorption and obsessive self-marketing. What should those who have pasted images of themselves all over the Internet anticipate? Who can deny that most teenagers and pre-teens have placed themselves on social sites to be viewed by anyone and everyone in the world? As we noted earlier, the traditional time frames for feedback required by earlier generations simply do not work today. How could we not have anticipated that instantaneous "intimacies" would develop in otherwise complicated social interactions? Simply stated, living lives in this time compression has resulted in the oblivion of patience. From *res ipsa* evidence alone, patience, especially as evident in youth, appears not to be a hardwired brain condition. Traditionally, being patient for the crop to be harvested or waiting patiently for a visitor coming by bus or airplane is no longer the vigil it once was. Could it be patience is learned along with PFC maturity?

YOUNG, BEAUTIFUL, AND NAÏVE

Recently, some journalists have use words such as *individualism* and *selfishness* to reflect on our preferred terms of *narcissism* and *self-absorbed entitlement,* which for some advance into corruption and beyond that to arrogance. Individualism and selfishness fail to deliver the psychological punch of clinical strength narcissism bordering on arrogance and grandiose varieties of grandiosity, which, in our argument, have progressively created a new version of sapient brains—a major adaptive rewiring of adolescent brains taking fewer than 50 years.

Psychological narcissism and behavioral entitlement suggest an increase in gradational strength of the chemistry that lies behind what the world inaccurately terms psychopathy to define today's young "movers and shakers." Increasingly, the adolescent version of moderate gradations of the spectrum suggests adolescents are more likely to raise their parents to their standards of immediacy rather than the reverse. That is, the traditional way of parents raising adolescent children to their standards of patience has given way to parents succumbing to the adolescent ideal of instant gratification.

The near abandonment of family values has been the predictable outcome of narcissistic self-aggrandizement, fostering the abandonment of accountability. Increasingly, young females become prey for violent predators who routinely manipulate, bully, abuse, or kill the naïve, a lesson memorialized by Ted Bundy when he said of his brutally murdered prey, "They were beautiful but naïve." As a reminder from an earlier chapter, prey are routinely blindsided by a major tool of evolution's deceptive practices—the guise of a charming male, personified in the childhood story of Prince Charming. Society's most elusive predators—sexually psychopathic serial killers—have been around a long time. The discipline of forensic investigative science has to evolve the ability to discover intraspecies predators.

American society appears to be ignoring the staple of formerly important issues. Have quality of education, wholesome family values, and the decent treatment of women and children declined in priority since the 1950s—a time closely aligned to the administration of Dwight Eisenhower? To anyone old enough to have lived in another time, it is *res ipsa* evident that America in the 1950s was not the same place it is today. The last president to be born in the 19th century, Eisenhower presided over our country during a period of time some would call the "good old days." The modern world has surely changed, but as we continue to note, those changes are nothing our sapient brains cannot handle. Today, as financial conundrums mount, with defense budgets ballooning and the national debt soaring out of control, the White House and Congress face monumental deadlines for budget reform. In 2011, even with an 11th-hour budget approval, Standard and Poor downgraded America's credit score to AA+. As a result, congressional disapproval soared to 82 percent (*Fort Worth Star-Telegram*, August 6, 2011). Yet through all the setbacks, political scandals, wars, and financial disgraces, we continue to survive individually and as a country. Survival seems certain. On what terms we will survive seems to be the only unknown part of the formula.

Are American dads as inept and cartoonish in real life as the dads in *Family Guy* and *The Simpsons*? It's just comedy, entertainment writers suggest. Likewise, are national leaders perceived as moderate opportunists ready and willing to scam millions of dollars in corruption reinforcing Washington, D.C.'s reputation? Is it business as usual? In realizing America is nothing like it was over 60 years ago, must traditional family values and education become diminished? No matter what "spin doctors" use in national politics to convince voters and the general public to gravitate one way or the other, we offer this bit of wisdom: There are lies, damn lies, and statistics. We will never get accurate statistics from anyone, especially politicians.

Here's another chilling question: Are we long past the apex of sapient brain achievement regarding class acts? Have we lost our grip on what it means for other countries to look to America for answers and as a beacon for hope? "The world looks to America," Peggy Noonan (*Wall Street Journal,* July 9, 2011) states, "It does not want to be patronized or dominated by America, it wants to see America as a beacon, an example, a dream of what could be. And the world wants something else: American goodness. It wants to have faith in the knowledge that America is the great nation that tries to think about and act upon right and wrong, and that it is a beacon also of things practical—how to have sturdy, good, unsoiled economy, how to create jobs that provide livelihoods that allow families to be formed, how to maintain a system in which inventors and innovators can flourish. A world without America in this sense—the beacon, the inspiration, the speaker of truth—would be a world deprived of hopefulness."

It is our argument that our deepest human problems become realities due to vigorous brain conditions—not personality disorders or false dichotomies of nature versus nurture that harken back to the pre-neuroscience decades of ego and personality psychology. We enter the world due to brain conditions, achieve or destroy ourselves and others while living the human condition, and die trying to adapt just one more time to the conditions of old age.

Sapient brains are primed by powerful endogenous chemical cascades that fire up in modular cerebral pathways as the authors of moods, emotions, thinking, and, ultimately, behavior. Marked by our choices, our perceptions, our social influences and experiences, and, most powerfully, our own individualized biological inheritance, *all* sapient brains are marked by the chemistry behind spectrum chemical gradations. Now more than ever, we must grow up as a species to the realities of neurotruths.

A startling example of surviving with tenacious and resilient resolve is evident in the life of Jaycee Lee Dugard, who was kidnapped at a bus stop as a young girl. Certainly night and day differences, the adaptive version of the sapient produced a hero of majestic proportions in Jaycee while the pathological version produced her conniving tormentors, Phillip Garrido and his wife (see chapter 6). Brain conditions work with chemical variations cascading across continua. For example, high-gain dopamine is known to produce the severe thought disorder schizophrenia (and Tourette syndrome), while DA in scarcity produces the neuromuscular condition of Parkinson's disease. Also, too much insulin produces diabetes, while scarcity results in hypoglycemia. From the 1990s forward, neuroscience has skyrocketed in providing information about our sapient brains.

TOFFLER'S *FUTURE SHOCK*

In his 1970 book *Future Shock,* sociologist and futurist Alvin Toffler defined *future shock* as "too much change in too short a period of time creat[ing] unprecedented anxieties of perception." Being a sociologist, the eternal search for social and cultural contingencies to shape behavior comprised Toffler's writing as a futurist. However, we contend that the mix of technological wizardry in mass communication and mass self-marketing, forging the oblivion of patience from anticipation of immediate gratification, has shown beyond doubt the power of adaptation in cortical tissue. A question that remains haunting in this chapter is this: Have gradations of what the world calls psychopathy led directly to an increase in sexual crimes and so-called wealth-management crimes? As side effects, might the devaluation of family values create a society with increases in corruptive and sexually predatory crimes?

Today our relationships are indeed cosmopolitan, but they are also transient, unpredictable, and often anonymous, even when engaged in for weeks or months. As the old-school personality psychologists used to ask, How long does it take to discover the real person lying beneath persona? In the midst of all this, the family—the once solid rock of nurturing—has practically vanished for many. Once, intimacy was measured in gradation over time. Permanence, predictability, and trust were cemented by proven performance across lengthy time frames. Today, extended families often crater after a few years, while nuclear families are shrinking in numbers as parents spend less time with preschool children. Even long-lasting marriages (those over 20 years) often weaken under the pressure of raising today's incredibly needy teenagers. Adolescents and young adults who have progeny soon discover the time drain is just too much and too demanding. Who steps up? Unfairly, aging grandparents often fill the void. In the age of pseudo-celebrity, social media devotees, and addicts, who has time to care about infants?

A study published by the UK's Basic Skills Agency notes that teachers have observed a side effect of neglect. Half of all children start school unable to speak audibly, be understood by others, respond to instructions, or even count to five. Videos and computer games are often used to entertain children in classrooms. Guidance is unwelcomed under conditions of acting out in class, and guidance does not mesh well with our "hot second" gratification time frame. What should such neglectful parents expect to occur in their children's emotional lives? Children put a constant drag on the attention of young parents, who believe they could be engaged in social networking sites instead of changing a smelly diaper or shoveling formula into the mouths of screaming kids. Such parents, as they attempt to talk face to face with their teenagers, grow impatient themselves. In the absence of real-time experiences that take longer than a few seconds, adolescents and young adults appear desperately needy for instantaneous attention from anyone, including online strangers.

Overall, traditional family values and a focus on obtaining a good education in preparation for launching successful careers appear to be rapidly disappearing in North America. On the rise, however, are narcissism and entitlement, represented by instant intimacies in anticipation of instant gratification, truly characteristic of modern teenage and young adult lives desperately seeking stimulation and perhaps validity.

MAKING THE CASE FOR THE DIFFERENTLY-ABLED I: STEVE JOBS (1955–2011)

Steve Jobs

adaptive   passionate achiever   maladaptive

|_____|_____|

survivors   thrivers   corruptive   pathological

The term *magical thinking,* long a staple in psychiatry and clinical psychology, is commonly defined as an erroneous belief that thoughts, words, or actions will cause a specific outcome defying the commonly understood laws of cause and effect. Maybe the problem with the current definition of magical thinking is that it is self-limiting and old school, specifically relating to the commonly understood laws of cause and effect. We contend that maybe the "laws" are deficient or out of step with modern neuroscience. What about individuals who are differently-abled for reasons not currently fully understood? The world is coming to appreciate Steve Jobs's version of magical thinking, known to Apple employees as his *reality distortion field*—a term from the original *Star Trek* television show. In Jobs's version of reality, magical thinking is the centerpiece. Jobs sincerely felt he could bend anything his way, evident in his most famous advertisement after returning to Apple. In his famous "Think different" TV ad, an off-camera voice says, "Here's to the crazy ones. The misfits. The rebels. The troublemakers. . . . And while some may see them as the crazy ones, we see genius. Because the people who are crazy enough to think they can change the world, are the ones who do."

Steve Jobs defines the modern zone of adaptive chemistry, which is punctuated by tenacity, resilience, and passion for what one believes. He revolutionized how we think and communicate. Just imagine how Jobs refined our brains with his bold vision.

MAKING THE CASE FOR THE DIFFERENTLY-ABLED II: CHESLEY BURNETT "SULLY" SULLENBERGER III (1951–)

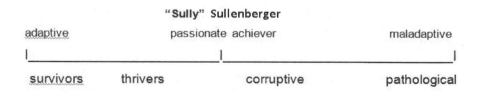

One way of looking at this might be that for forty-two years, I've been making small, regular deposits in this bank of experience: education and training. And on January 15, the balance was sufficient so that I could make a very large withdrawal.

Sully Sullenberger, *60 Minutes,* February 8, 2009

By occupation, Chesley "Sully" Sullenberger was an American airline transport pilot, safety expert, and accident investigator. On January 15, 2010, a little over a week from his 58th birthday, he successfully landed U.S. Airways Flight 1549 in the Hudson River near Manhattan, saving the lives of all 155 people aboard the aircraft (Sullenberger 2009).

On March 2, 2010, he retired from U.S. Airways after 30 years as a commercial pilot. He is now an on-air aviation expert for CBS News and author of *Highest Duty* (2009), a memoir of his life and the circumstances surrounding Flight 1549. In *Time* magazine's 2009 "Top 100 Most Influential Heroes and Icons," he ranked second on the list.

Speaking about the ordeal of ditching his plane, Sully said, "It was very quiet as we worked, my co-pilot and I. We were a team. But to have zero thrust coming out of those engines was shocking—the silence" *(ESPN: The Magazine,* February 6, 2009). He has acknowledged a short bout of post-traumatic stress disorder symptoms following the landing, but said the condition receded fairly quickly.

In less spectacular ways, individuals "step up" in times of emergency with skills and courage. Prepared by education and experience, Sully Sullenberger displayed courage and a vigorous brain finely tuned to the middle of the neurospectrum—reserved for those who live lives of passion and dedication.

Chapter 11

The Rise of Neurotruth

READERS' PRE-TEST

Neurotruth is composed of

a. neurology
b. genetics
c. experiences
d. behavioral habits and patterns
e. evolutionary development
f. scientific facts
g. all of the above

The answer is *g,* all of the above.

LIFE IS A BALANCING ACT

This pivotal chapter brings together threads of our argument that psychopathy is indeed on the same neurospectrum as life-affirming chemistry. Indeed, *life is a balancing act.* In part 1 of this book, we presented in four chapters discussions of how psychopathy, born of ancient brain conditions, can become perverted by arrogance and thus maladaptive to living in social harmony. Truly, psychopathy is entrenched in North American culture, but so is thriving, surviving, and passionate achieving. Further evidence emerged in parts 2 and 3, with details of the modern neurospectrum and how effortlessly charming and handsome psychopaths spin cocoons around females who are tragically blindsided by their *je ne sais quoi.*

In behavioral neuroscience, the hard science pedigree of neuropsychology, in which brain science is merged with neurology and forensic investigative science, everything is a clue. Clues are ripe for the taking, observed in body language, tone of voice, and mannerisms, all of which announce vigorous brain conditions at work, producing the differently-abled as the defining ingredient of our wondrous species. By engaging neurotruth, forensic investigative scientists will be far more effective than in previous generations.

Now more than ever before, scientists and laypeople alike are equipped to recognize the significance held by the gift of gab, narcissism, entitlement, and the appearance of arrogance and grandiose arrogance—the latter being the most significant behavioral clue that deceptive practices have given way to sexualized violence seen in rapacious rapists and murderers.

When individuals become aware others are watching them, they often change demeanor and begin to audition. We don't always know for what, but we can observe the behavioral clues: Flashy personas and smiling faces often suggest the predator within another person might just be priming us . . . but for what? If we hang around long enough, we're sure to find out. However, we must realize up front that first impressions are often deceiving.

EIGHTEEN BEHAVIORAL NEUROTRUTHS FOR THE 21ST CENTURY

- *Neurotruth 1.* From birth, female sapient brains are mandated by vigorous brain conditions—configured from ancient survival scripts, reflected in gender differences, and reinforced by social experiences—to do almost anything for love. Procuring the experience of love is a top priority of the female brain. In common parlance, females are "love junkies," forever in search of Mr. Right.
- *Neurotruth 2.* From birth, male sapient brains are mandated by vigorous brain conditions—configured from ancient survival scripts, reflected in gender differences, and reinforced by social experiences—to do almost anything for sex. Procuring a consistent sexual experience is a top priority of the male brain. In common parlance, males are "sex junkies" searching for willing partners.
- *Neurotruth 3.* Female sapient brains are vulnerable to the charms of handsome males. Possessing a gift of gab, he weaves his web of lies and half-truths around her in a masterful deception. Consequently, she feels love and imagines family. This excitatory experience is rooted in fast-acting, pair-bonding cascades of oxytocin in addition to DANE brain and PEA brain

enhanced by testosterone and estrogen and boosted by the youthful exuberance of DHEA and beta-endorphin. Females risk abuse and other terrors from corruptive and pathological psychopaths who blindside them with charm and good looks.

- *Neurotruth 4.* Male sapient brains stimulated on sight to sexual stimulation from female hormone markers are vulnerable on sight to sexual inspiration from female hormone markers (her face, lips, hair, breasts, waist, legs, etc.), either in singular parts or in select combinations. In her initial response, she is blinded by the attention lavished upon her, so that none of his behaviors appear threatening. Cascades of DHEA, DANE brain, and PEA brain, turbocharged by testosterone, rush through his brain as he starts the seduction audition, which masks his ultimate goal of manipulation and control—a proclivity of male brains. Immediately upon seeing an attractive female, he's thinking one thing—sexual adventure—while she's sizing him up as a future mate. Deception is made so much easier due to this halo effect of excitatory chemistry cascading and defining sexual attraction. The male initiates the audition by visually paying attention to her, locking eyes, and accentuating his charming smile. That's all it takes.

- *Neurotruth 5.* A level playing field for female sapient brains versus male varieties requires the female to lead with her trump card—her emotional and sexual DANE brainmark. Emotional drama, generated from ancient survival scripts, empowers the female to win her side of any argument by deploying her version of special weapons and tactics—tears, jeers, screams, deception, throwing an occasional object, or sex. The female sapient brain is masterful at creating human drama, which often trumps the male's futile replies.

- *Neurotruth 6.* Across all relationships, females tend to pair bond too quickly, refusing to budge once a potential Mr. Right has been found. As evidence builds that her choice is less Mr. Right and more Mr. Very Wrong, she relies on female intuition (which she trusts explicitly) enhanced by DANE brainmarks, PEA brainmarks, and quick-acting oxytocin, solidifying her largely emotional choice. Sealed by her SANE brainmark, liberated serotonin "factually" guaranteeing her unwavering devotion, her final strategy emerges: She can and will change him.

- *Neurotruth 7.* The strong emotions of love, willpower, and hope reside in sapient brains due to tenacity and resilience born of cascades of excitatory endogenous chemistry, precursors to these deeply felt human emotions. All three are transformational emotions that ignite change, motivation, and devotion in adapting to new strategies and energies in the attainment of social harmony and pair bonding in loving and committed relationships. We are not a weak and vulnerable species, but we are often naïve until we learn fundamental lessons about human relationships. We are not prone to disorder and dysfunction, as many, if not most, clinical psychologists and psychiatrists perceive us to be. The truth is, we are endowed with powerful, life-affirming chemistry.

- *Neurotruth 8.* Males are primed by ancient survival scripts to be territorial predators competing for sexual favors, while females are primed by nature and cortical connectivity to be nurturers and communicators, thus configuring the universal yin-yang of female-male differences, which emerge as magnets of attraction. Strong survival abilities, observed as tenacity and resilience, combined with the laser focus of hope (something to look forward to) and strengthened by strong reward chemistry from tender emotional expressions (love) become permanent brainmarks in our memory (via the hypothalamus).

- *Neurotruth 9.* Male and female sapient brains are primed by powerful chemistry, hormones, and neuroglia to influence others by attentive flirting, articulated as auditioning. Pretense is everywhere in this evolutionarily mandated process. Males audition for sex, while females audition for love (and in the process, sex). Enter deception as a cloud of doubt consuming the participants. Every molecule in her body is focused on his attention as the precursor to, perhaps, a deeper involvement. He becomes her obsession. In her mind, he is Mr. Right, and she feels compelled to make her move, mindful of the competitors circling around her like vultures. But patience is exceedingly important in correctly identifying behavioral auditions from those who seek to engage us. The challenge becomes to see "cracks in the foundation"—the deception masking compulsive liars. Patience gives those in the audience more time to read the subtle clues given off by those who are performing.

- *Neurotruth 10.* Human touch, as well as physical activity of almost any kind, is required for normal brain development. Without physical activity tightly packing the cerebellum, social and pair bonding are compromised. Purchasing a trampoline (with a safety net) and and participating in youth sports (especially noncontact sports such as gymnastics and volleyball) offer parents the best strategies for helping their children and adolescents become more brain healthy and thus enhancing cerebral development, which results in early advantages in learning and socialization.

- *Neurotruth 11.* The adolescent developmental phase of life, characterized by the adolescent brain's dive into deceptive practices with a prodigious amount of lying and cover-up, represents a supreme challenge to parents. It is a foundational neurotruth that when antecedent behavior produces pleasing and rewarding payoffs—so that behavior is shaped and maintained by its consequences—the behavior is going to be repeated, regardless of the deception it takes to repeat it. Thus adolescence is the most dangerous and confusing developmental stage of life due to the discovery of the laws of behavioral payoffs. The day-to-day challenges, even for well-informed and involved parents, can be exhausting. Drawing deep lines in the sand, and loading those lines with consequences, is just about the best strategic plan for raising hardheaded children.

- *Neurotruth 12.* What the world erroneously refers to as psychopathy is actually a by-product of a vigorous brain condition powered by cascades of endogenous chemistry. These powerful neurotransmitters and neuroglia make up the 70–80 percent of life-affirming, adaptive chemistry on the neurospectrum, a stark contrast to the 20–30 percent of the spectrum reflecting life-corrupting and violent life-destructive maladaptive brain conditions. Vigorous brain conditions known as psychopathy are driven by perversions of excitatory, inhibitory, and neuroglia activities and exacerbated by deviant neurocognitive mapping, toxic parenting, and other influences still the topic of scientific debate.

- *Neurotruth 13.* A powerful perversity in chemical cascades is hypothesized to account for vigorous brain conditions becoming corruptive to the extent that larcenous behavior results. Such psychopathic behavior can be characterized as a rise in arrogance, which produces, at least, criminal behavior and, at most, violent and sexualized predatory behavior, as seen in pathological psychopathy in severe cases of maladaptation. Grandiose arrogance is the most severe example of violent maladaptation in our species. It is a foundational neurotruth in forensic investigative science that arrogance in corruptive versions and grandiose arrogance in violence-laced predatory versions account for 20–30 percent of the varieties of the neurospectrum. Both versions are deserving of the clinical diagnosis of psychopathy.

- *Neurotruth 14.* Excitatory DANE brain—dopamine and norepinephrine—compounded by the amphetamine-like PEA brain represent excitatory chemical cascades responsible for experiencing life-affirming rewards from "pleasure molecules." Excitatory chemistry is transformational, producing euphoric and exhilarating experiences engineered from ancient survival scripts. Innovators and achievers find their own brands of passion from the same chemistry which turbocharges their drive, work ethic, and motivation to attain highly acclaimed careers.

- *Neurotruth 15.* Inhibitory SANE brain (from liberated serotonin) and GABA brain (from gamma aminobutyric acid liberation) act to chemically balance excitatory DANE (dopamine and norepinephrine liberation) and PEA (phenylethylamine), allowing restraint and producing more harmonious gradations of cool, calm, and collected confidence. Without inhibitory chemistry, it would be impossible to rest and feel rejuvenated by a good night's sleep. In fact, inhibitory brainmarks are just as important, if not more so, for rest and rejuvenation than excitatory versions.

- *Neurotruth 16.* Adolescents are vulnerable to making bad choices due to tendencies toward impulsivity and the dominance of DANE brain exacerbated by slowly developing prefrontal cortexes—the brain region most dependent upon experiences and therefore the last to develop as the agent of cognitive reconsideration. Hence, adolescents and prefrontal parents are often not in the same brain regions when it comes to communication and decision making. Adolescents are awash in midbrain limbic sentimentalities, characterized by emotions and sexuality in immature relationships, explaining the almost continuous episodes of drama and angst. Numerous developmental studies have shown that the PFC regions of the frontal lobes do not become connected enough for mature cognitive reconsideration until the late 20s to mid-30s. Weakly performing PFCs account for the predominance of spur-of-the-moment decisions that characterize adolescents. If not for parents demanding responsibilities as a continuous priority, one bad decision after another would dominate adolescent behavior. This neurotruth is a nightmare for parents who can't seem to get their hardheaded children to see their side of an argument. Separated by mere cortical inches, adult truths are simply not compatible with adolescent adventures.

- *Neurotruth 17.* In modern evolutionary neuropsychology, the classical term *natural selection* refers to powerful brain conditions produced via neurotransmitters and neuroglia, assisted by hormones from the endocrine system and replenished by gastrointestinal microbes. This process assures that helpful traits are not only retained in gene pools but also function as lifelong and continuous brainmarks. No human conditions exist that are more powerful than the basic brainmarks, two of which are excitatory (DANE and PEA, amplified by DHEA and testosterone), two of which are inhibitory (SANE and GABA), and one of which is analgesic (beta-endorphin). It is currently unknown specifically what cause-and-effect indicators allow corruptive and pathological versions to compromise otherwise adaptive gradations across the neurospectrum. Strong genetic proclivities, predispositions, vulnerabilities, and addictions are suspected to lead to perversion and pathology.
- *Neurotruth 18.* The reality of "acting out" means sapient-brained individuals of all ages and developmental stages do exactly what they want to do (or think they want to do) when they want to do it. It has been said a person is fortunate to have a few trusted friends who can be relied upon to tell them the truth. People have a tendency to befriend those who share similar perceptions and values. It's up to us to remember that all behaviors, from tone of voice to facial expressions (or lack thereof), are clues. As we get older and continue to make new acquaintances, we continually find ourselves asking this question: I wonder what that person is really like?

LIE TO ME: CONTEMPLATING NEUROTRUTHS

Psychologist Paul Ekman (portrayed by actor Tim Roth in the TV series *Lie to Me*) spent his entire career observing facial *microexpressions,* tied to brain conditions, across many continents and cultures. Today, after more than two decades of image-based brain research, augmented by Ekman's earlier work, the expanding field of behavioral neuroscience has become a worldwide discipline. To our initial list of 18 neurotruths, the coming years should add hundreds more in other publications. For those not persuaded by neuroscience, still faithfully clinging to old-school psychiatry and clinical psychology and their insistence upon finding disorder, dysfunction, and disease from the pages of the DSM, we recommend you read just one book to solidify our perspective, Cummings and O'Donohue's *Eleven Blunders that Cripple Psychotherapy in America* (2008).

As noted in the preceding chapters, we are not a flawed species in the least; we are vulnerable to all kinds of chemical imbalances that require clinical diagnoses for "damaged" affect, personality (whatever that is), and all varieties of disorders and dysfunctions from infancy to old age. One final neurotruth seals the deal in our estimation of the human condition and the role of adaptive gradations of what the world calls psychopath: Our species is far more adaptive than maladaptive. Otherwise, we would have gone the way of the dinosaurs long ago.

MAKING THE CASE FOR THE DIFFERENTLY-ABLED I: TED TURNER (1938–)

Ted Turner

adaptive	passionate achiever	maladaptive

survivors	thrivers	corruptive	pathological

In 1970, Robert Edward "Ted" Turner III started his ambitious career in broadcasting by purchasing an Atlanta UHF station and launching it as Turner Broadcasting System (TBS). Along the way, everything he touched turned to gold: the Atlanta Braves baseball team (1976), the Goodwill Games (1986), World Championship Wrestling, and the Turner Network Television channel. Turner founded the first 24-hour news channel, CNN, in 1980 (*Encyclopedia Britannica,* 15th ed., s.v. "Ted Turner"). Regarding the continuity of his creation, Turner stated, "We won't be signing off until the world ends. We'll be on and we'll cover the end of the world, live, and that will be our last event. We'll play nearer my God to thee and then sign off" (CNN, "Ted Turner: The Maverick Man," November 23, 2102). Turner also founded the superstation concept of cable news with Atlanta station WTBS. Philanthropically, his gift of $1 billion to support the United Nations created a new public charity, the United Nations Foundation.

In his early years, Turner was expelled from Brown University, where he was studying economics, and was denied his diploma for having a female student in his dorm. In 1989, he was awarded an honorary bachelor of arts degree when he delivered the keynote address on his former campus. A prodigious sailor, he defended the America's Cup in 1977 by defeating a team from Australia. Turner's three failed marriages have produced five children. He is currently one of the largest landowners in the nation, as his prolific purchases have secured 15 ranches spanning six states (*Encyclopedia Britannica,* 15th ed., s.v. "Ted Turner").

MAKING THE CASE FOR THE DIFFERENTLY-ABLED II: ELIOT NESS (1903–1957)

With a master's degree in criminology, Eliot Ness set out to make his mark in life. He joined the U.S. Treasury Department in 1927 and was appointed to the Bureau of Prohibition in Chicago. With the election of President Herbert Hoover and help from the Secret Six—a group of influential Chicago businessmen—master gangster Al Capone was targeted as a crime boss who had to be brought to justice. To "get his man," Ness charged Capone with tax evasion (he had failed to pay income taxes on his illegal breweries during Prohibition). Due to Capone's hold on the city, which included payoffs to corrupt law enforcers, Ness handpicked his own men—11 in all—who along with Ness became known as the "Untouchables." Ignoring assassination attempts on his life, Ness and the Untouchables began closing down illegal stills and breweries thanks to wire tapping leads (Encyclopedia Britannica, 15th ed., s.v. "Eliot Ness").

In the end, Ness had little to do with the legal proceedings against Capone; he acted mostly as a smokescreen to Frank K. Wilson, the accountant who found $17,000 of income collected at Capone's Hawthorn Smoke Shop, where no taxes were paid. This fact was verified by Capone's bookkeeper, Leslie Shumway, who was also targeted for assassination but lived to testify against Capone on behalf of the FBI, thus sealing the case. Capone was found guilty and sentenced to 11 years in prison. Thus ended his reign of crime and terror in Chicago, but not before the jury was switched at the last minute when it was discovered Capone had paid to influence the first jury.

Ness gave author Oscar Fraley 21 pages of notes, which the author used to write the book *The Untouchables* (1957), the basis for the popular TV series starring Robert Stack (1959–1963). A number of TV shows and movies over the years have also been made, including Brian De Palma's Oscar-winning movie adaptation *The Untouchables* (1987), starring Kevin Costner as Ness and Robert De Niro as psychopath Al Capone.

Like Capone, Ness was indeed differently-abled—but as an achiever in protecting society from corruption at a difficult time in our history. The contrast of Ness versus Capone is telling, as both were in the middle zone of gradational strengths, Ness on the life-affirming side and Capone on the life-destroying side.

Epilogue

Corruptive Psychopaths

READERS' PRE-TEST

In the final analysis, a psychopath

a. has strong genetic propensities to be psychopathic
b. has inherited biological predispositions to be psychopathic
c. has toxic experiences with parenting that can exacerbate both *a* and *b*
d. displays early behavioral manifestations of psychopathy that are often ignored
e. poses special problems for the female brain—a brain searching for connection, intimacy, and bonding
f. all of the above

The answer is *f*, all of the above.

> *I think the madness business is filled with people . . . reduced to their maddest edges. Some . . . are locked up in units for scoring too high on Bob [Hare's] checklist. Others are on TV at nine p.m., their dull, ordinary, non-mad attributes skillfully edited out, benchmarks of how we shouldn't be. There are obviously a lot of very ill people out there.* But there are also people in the middle, getting over-labeled, becoming nothing more than a big splurge of madness in the minds of people who benefit from it [emphasis added].

(Ronson 2011, 267)

This epilogue brings the curtain down on our investigation into the amazing neurospectrum of chemical and cortical templates configuring sapient brains and the story of how psychopathy can manifest itself. As we have seen, psychopathy is not a personality disorder and it never has been. Nor is it a version of psychosis (or insanity) or related to schizophrenia. It's a scenario of maladaptation and perversion of what could have been a differently-abled life.

What transpires from our potent mix of genetics and experiences speaks volumes for adaptability and how our species comes equipped to survive and thrive and even become passionate achievers. Born of genetics and fashioned from the twin social influences of parenting and peers, corruption and pathology drive a hard bargain for those seeking normalcy. With the advent of the Decade of the Brain (1990–1999), we can peer inside the cranium to view a living brain—a brain that can be normal, achieving, corruptive, criminal, or psychopathic. Our insistence upon applying neurotruth is testimony to the contribution of modern neuroscience in this regard. Neurotruth (Jacobs 2011) speaks volumes for the value of paying attention to red flags and how they can make visible the invisible in one's motivations. As a species, we will always have corruptive bottom-feeders hiding in wait, like trapdoor spiders, just as there will always be passionate achievers who love life and soar above the masses with creative influences that change the world and make it a more interesting place to live. Our evolutionary history guarantees that. Our argument and perspective, that vigorous brain conditions lie behind our powerful brainmarks, is supported by neuroscience, a plethora of research, and psychometric verification in Hare's Psychopathy Checklist-Revised. All of those individuals with lower scores on the PCL-R must be measuring the test takers who choose to live lives of responsibility in social harmony with consequences squarely in mind. Likewise, a variety of academic books support our notion of variations and varieties of psychopathic-like traits that lead to achievement (Hare 1993, 2003; Kantor 2006; Raine and Sanmartin 2001).

To operate with the best chance of acquiring successes, sapient brains appear to require something to believe in, something to look forward to—sustaining "tonics" to keep the cerebral embers of motivation and emotion stoked. The human condition is a powerful reminder of our lofty position atop the food chain. In the preceding chapters, we explored the powerful endogenous chemistry that animates the amazing neurospectrum of life-affirming chemistry as well as life-defeating varieties that predictably lead to downward spirals.

We identified the powerful chemistry behind everyday survivors, individuals who are able to adapt to real issues of living with tenacity and resilience as adolescents and young adults while others barely hang by a thread of hope, driven by willpower and the belief things will change.

Contrastingly, in instances of maladaptation, multiple layers of toxicity are exposed as brainmarks primed to produce societal monsters. What else but our individualized DNA, exacerbated by toxic relationships, could accomplish such transformations? Addiction, toxic or disengaged parenting, and other psychological deficiencies remain the most likely candidates for the appearance of arrogance in the flesh-and-blood monsters who feel entitled to do what they desire, stoked by perverted erotic cognitive mapping. The monstrous vulgarities of Ottis Toole and the vicious sexual sadism of Paul Bernardo, Karla Homolka, and Ted Bundy make shockingly clear the reason for the psychopathy's place on the neurospectrum of severity regarding pathological monsters. In sum, and split down the moderate middle, the adaptives go to the left and the maladaptives go to the right. Greed's corruption into larcenous self-obsession propels the arrogant into wrecking financial futures, but their behaviors are nothing compared to the monstrous perversion of violence that often seem gothic and surreal— the crime scenes of sexual forensics. To become educated to the red flags of the developing Mr. Hyde behind the respectable Dr. Jekyll alerts researchers and investigators to the dark and destructive side of pathological psychopathy.

But before we address the monster's red flags, we wish to tie up some loose ends from preceding chapters. Incredibly, we all start with roughly the same neurochemistry, which becomes articulated in vigorous brainmarks as the chemistry behind our idiosyncratic behavior. To a pair of early pioneers in the FBI, Robert Ressler and John Douglas, who ventured into prison lockups to interview the worst of the worst, we owe a debt of gratitude for what they discovered. Their known-offender characteristics are a source for information on arrogant, criminal minds. The aforementioned FBI research has been shown, even before the dawning of neuroscience, that none of the varieties across the 20–30 percent of the psychopathy spectrum, absent severe mental incapacitation, suffer in the least. Rather, they feel empowered, entitled, and bulletproof, especially when saturated by arrogance, anger, and retribution. These are the psychopaths—the corruptively and pathologically differently-abled—who will steal your money and even your life, and never look back. That's the life they choose, and that's the life they feel most comfortable with.

RED FLAGS OF ANTISOCIAL CRIMINALS AND PSYCHOPATHS

Antisocial criminals are as a rule not charming, handsome, or highly intelligent, but they may exhibit some psychopathic traits. These monsters feel entitled to fulfill their desires without empathy or conscience. One only needs the gift of sight and a functional amygdala to avoid them. Though categorized as antisocial criminal types, they can nonetheless have psychopathic pedigrees. The complexities of the human condition speak volumes to the factors producing society's monsters. Severe mental issues, toxic and disengaged parenting, addiction, and severe abuses can combine in psychopathy and antisocial criminal behavior. Unfortunately, diagnosis is not always as cut and dried as the DSM's concept of differential diagnoses suggests. Monsters come in all shapes and sizes, often showing the world Dr. Jekyll and sparing them Mr. Hyde, but the clock is ticking and the time will come when the monster comes out of hiding. We conclude by presenting 2 final examples who make our case for the "differently-abled," examples that will be hard to forget considering how much they could have elevated their lives—if only.

MAKING THE CASE FOR THE DIFFERENTLY-ABLED I: BERNARD MADOFF (1938–)

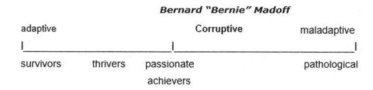

Bernard "Bernie" Madoff

adaptive   Corruptive   maladaptive

survivors   thrivers   passionate   pathological
                              achievers

The nature of any human being, certainly anyone on Wall Street, is the better deal you give the customer, the worse deal it is for you.

Bernard Madoff

Bernard "Bernie" Madoff, former stockbroker, investor, and admitted operator of a massive Ponzi scheme, considered the largest financial fraud in American history, pleaded guilty in 2009 to 11 federal felonies as "wealth manager" for trusting investors he bilked out of billions, perhaps as much as $65 billion. In December 2008, Madoff's sons (not Madoff himself) disclosed to authorities that the assets management unit of his company, according to their father, was one "one big lie" (*Washington Post,* December 13, 2008). He was arrested the next day and charged with securities fraud. Previously, the Securities and Exchange Commission (SEC) had investigated his business practices but found nothing amiss to suggest mismanagement.

The arrogance of Madoff was documented in 2002, when he referred to incompetent SEC investigators (from six investigations) as "Lieutenant Colombos" who never asked the right questions (*New York Daily News,* October 31, 2009). In June 2009, he was sentenced to 150 years in prison, where he remains today, as arrogant as ever. In 2010, Mark Madoff, one of his sons, committed suicide by hanging himself.

MAKING THE CASE FOR THE DIFFERENTLY-ABLED II: ROD BLAGOJEVICH (1956–)

Rod Blagojevich

adaptive		Corruptive	maladaptive
survivors	thrivers	passionate achievers	pathological

After a barrage of lies proclaiming his innocence from the beginning, at sentencing, Rod "Blago" Blagojevich finally became transparent long enough to admit guilt: "I've made terrible mistakes. My life is ruined now. My political career is over and I can't be a lawyer any more. We can't afford the home we life in, we're trying to sell it" (Bury 2011). After facing the music, finally admitting guilt, and making prodigious apologies before the presiding judge, Blago's sentence was announced on December 7, 2011. The impeached former governor of Illinois and former attorney, was sentenced to 14 years in federal prison and disbarment. He had been found guilty in August 2010 of lying to the FBI and guilty of 17 out of 20 counts of federal corruption.

The guilty verdict was the culmination of events that stemmed from Blagojevich's arrest on allegations of federal corruption, including conspiracy to commit mail and wire fraud and solicitation of bribery. The Justice Department alleged that "the governor conspired to commit several 'pay to play' schemes to obtain personal gain through corrupt use of his authority to fill Barack Obama's vacated U.S. Senate seat." In wire-tapped recordings, Blagojevich discussed his desire to get something in exchange for an appointment to Obama's vacant seat.

Under federal guidelines, Blagojevich must serve 12 years, or 85 percent of his sentence. Upon release he will be in his mid-60s. Prior to investigation for corruption, Rasmussen Reports ranked him as "America's Least Popular Governor" (partly based on a December 2011 article in the *Journal Star* by Andy Kravetz, "Area Attorneys Say Blagojevich Apology, Remorse Came Too Late").

In a long line of corrupt politicians, Blagojevich is yet another example of how arrogance is the driving force behind corruptive psychopathy and the willingness to hang on long enough in hopes that someone will start to believe the mountain of serial lies. Those of us who do academic research into psychopathic characteristics wonder when the famous doing the infamous will ever learn that liars are only tolerated when they become (apparently) humble and repent, temporarily (though deceptively) pushing the "pause" button on their self-entitled arrogance by admitting personal demons. Instead, they often do not appear sorry for their actions, just sorry they got caught. But a strategy of repentance, though it does not necessarily work for some (such as Richard Nixon or John Edwards), for others works miraculously. (In an earlier profile we observed a repentant President Clinton hanging by a thread in the highest political office in the land until he "fessed up.") As image is everything in American celebrity, the fall of someone such as Lance Armstrong was predictable. But what becomes of the fallen hero?

Bibliography

Ackerman, Diane. 2004. *An alchemy of mind: The marvel and mystery of the brain.* New York: Scribner.

Albert, Marilyn, and Guy McKhann. 2006. *Brain research: 2006 progressive report.* New York: Dana Press.

American Psychiatric Association (APA). 2000. *Diagnostic and statistical manual of mental disorders* (DSM-IV-TR). Washington, D.C.: American Psychological Association.

Aynesworth, Hugh. 1999. *The only living witness: The true story of serial sex killer Ted Bundy.* Irving, Tex.: Authorlink Press.

Babiak, Paul, and Robert D. Hare. 2006. *Snakes in suits: When psychopaths go to work.* New York: HarperCollins.

Barbaree, Howard. E., and William L. Marshall, eds. 2006. *The juvenile sex offender.* 2nd ed. New York: Guilford Press.

Barsam, Richard, and Dave Monahan. 2010. *Looking at movies: An introduction to film.* 3rd ed. New York: W. W. Norton.

Barton, Billy Bob. 1996. "An interview with Ottis Toole: The Cannibal Kid." *The Konformist.* http://www.konformist.com/2000/cannibal-kid.htm/.

Basic Skills Agency of the UK. http://www.skillsforlifenetwork.com/?atk=2530

Bear, Mark F., Barry W. Connors, and Michael A. Paradiso. 2006. *Neuroscience: Exploring the brain.* 3rd ed. Baltimore: Lippincott, Williams, & Wilkins.

Beatty, Jackson. 1995. *Principles of behavioral neuroscience.* Dubuque, Iowa: Brown & Benchmark.

Bienenstock J., Clarke G., Desbonnet L., Dinan T.G., Garrett L. 2008. "The probiotic bifidobacteria infantis: An assessment of potential antidepressant properties in the rat." *Journal of Psychiatric Research* 43, no. 2 (December): 164–74.

Blair, James, Derek Mitchell, and Karina Blair. 2005. *The psychopath: Emotion and the brain.* Oxford: Blackwell.

Blame It on Rio. 1984. Dir. Stanley Donen. Sherwood Productions.

Blank, Robert H. 1999. *Brain policy: How the new neuroscience will change our own lives and our politics.* Washington, D.C.: Georgetown University Press.

Boleyn-Fitzgerald, Miriam. 2010. *Picture of the mind: What the new neuroscience tells us about who we are.* Upper Saddle River, N.J.: Pearson Education.

Breggin, Peter D. 1991. *Toxic psychiatry: Why therapy, empathy, and love must replace the drugs, electroshock, and biochemical theories of the "new psychiatry."* New York: St. Martin's Press.

Brizendine, Louann. 2010. *The male brain: A breakthrough understanding of how men and boys think.* New York: Three Rivers Press.

Brizendine, Louann. 2006. *The female brain.* New York: Morgan Road Books.

Brown, Nina. 2006. *Coping with infuriating, mean, critical people: The destructive narcissistic pattern.* Westport, Conn.: Praeger.

Burnham, Terry, and Jay Phelan. 2000. *Mean genes.* New York: Perseus.

Bury, Chris. 2011. "Blagojevich sentenced to 14 years." *ABC News,* December 7. http://abcnews.go.com/blogs/headlines/2011/12/judgment-day-for-blagojevich/.

Canli, Turhan, ed. 2006. *Biology of personality and individual differences.* New York: Guilford Press.

Carpenter, Siri. 2012. "That gut feeling." *Monitor on Psychology* 43, no. 8 (September): 51.

Carr, Nicholas. 2010. *The shallows: What the Internet is doing to our brains.* London: W. W. Norton.

Changeux-Jean-Pierre. 1985. *Neuronal man: The biology of mind.* New York: Oxford University Press.

Cocca, Carolyn. 2006. *Adolescent sexuality: A historical handbook and guide.* Westport, Conn.: Praeger.

Cohen, Sidney. 1988. *The chemical brain: The neurochemistry of addictive disorders.* Irvine, Calif.: CareInstitute.

Colapinto, John. 2001. *As nature made him: The boy who was raised as a girl.* New York: Harper Perennial.

Colapinto, John. 1998. "The true story of John/Joan." *Rolling Stone,* December 11, 54–97.

Conrad, Mark T. 2006. "Symbolism, meaning, and nihilism in pulp fiction." In *The philosophy of film noir,* edited by Mark T. Conrad. Lexington: University Press of Kentucky.

Cooper, Jack R., Floyd E. Bloom, and Robert H. Roth. 2003. *The biochemical basis of neuropharmacology.* 8th ed. New York: Oxford University Press.

Cornwell, Patricia. 2002. *Portrait of a killer: Jack the ripper—case closed.* New York: G. P. Putnam's Sons.

Cummings, Nicholas A., and William T. O'Donohue. 2008. *Eleven blunders that cripple psychotherapy in America: A remedial unblundering.* New York: Routledge.

Damasio, Antonio. 1994. *Descartes' error: Emotion, reason, and the human brain.* New York: Penguin Books.

Dana Alliance for Brain Initiatives. 2010. *A neuroscientist's perspective on the advances in the genetics of psychiatric disorders: The 2010 progress report on brain research.* New York: Dana Press.

Dana Foundation. 2007. *Cerebrum: Emerging ideas in brain science.* New York: Dana Press.

Darby, David, and Kevin Walsh. 2005. *Neuropsychology: A clinical approach.* 5th ed. New York: Elsevier.

Darwin, Charles. 2009. *The origin of species.* 150th Anniversary Edition. 1859. Reprint, Alachua, Fla.: Bridge-Logos.

Dellesega, Cheryl. 2001. *Surviving Ophelia.* Cambridge, Mass.: Perseus Publishing.

Douglas, John. 1995. *Mind hunter: Inside the FBI's elite serial crime unit.* New York: Scribner.

Douglas, John, Ann W. Burgess, Allen G. Burgess, and Robert Ressler. 1992. *Crime classification manual: A standard system for investigating and classifying violent crime.* San Francisco: Jossey-Bass.

Douglas, John, and Mark Olshaker. 1999. *The anatomy of motive.* New York: Pocket Books.

Douglas, John, and Mark Olshaker. 1998. *Obsession.* New York: Pocket Books.

Dugard, Jaycee. 2011. *A stolen life: A memoir.* New York: Simon & Schuster.

Dutton, K. 2012. *The wisdom of psychopaths: What saints, spies, and serial killers can teach us about success.* New York: Scientific American/Farrar, Straus and Giroux.

Felson, Marcus. 2006. *Crime and nature.* Thousand Oaks, Calif.: Sage.

Festinger, L. 1957. *A theory of cognitive dissonance.* Stanford, California: Stanford University Press.

Fields, R. Douglas. 2011a. "The hidden brain." *Scientific American Mind* 22, no. 2 (May/June): 53–59.

Fields, R. Douglas. 2011b. *The other brain: The scientific and medical breakthroughs that will heal our brains and revolutionize our health.* New York: Simon & Schuster.

Fields, R. Douglas. 2010. "Change in the brain's white matter." *Science* 330 (November): 768–769.

Fields, R. Douglas. 2008. "White matter matters." *Scientific American* 298, no. 3 (March): 54–61.

Foley, James, dir. 1993. *Fear.* Imagine Entertainment, distributed by Universal Pictures.

Francis, Keith A. 2007. *Charles Darwin and The Origin of Species.* Westport, Conn.: Greenwood Press.

Garbarino, James. 1999. *Lost boys: Why our sons turn violent and how we can save them.* New York: Anchor Books.

Giedd, Jay, N. 2009. *The teenage brain: Primed to learn, primed to take risks.* New York: Dana Foundation.

Goldberg, Elkhonon. 2001. *The executive brain: Frontal lobes and the civilized mind.* New York: Oxford University Press.

Guthrie, Robert V. 2004. *Even the rat was white: An historical view of psychology.* New York: Pearson.

Hall, Alan. 2009. Office conversation with Professor Jacobs at Weatherford College.

Hallowell, Edward M., and John J. Ratey. 1994. *Driven to distraction: Recognizing and coping with attention deficit disorder from childhood through adulthood.* New York: Touchstone.

Hancock, Paul, and Brian Skinner, eds. 2000. *The Oxford companion to the Earth.* New York: Oxford University Press.

Hare, Robert D. 2003. The Hare psychopathy checklist-revised (PCL-R).

Hare, Robert D. 1993. *Without conscience: The disturbing world of the psychopaths among us.* New York: Guilford Press.

Harris, Thomas. 2000. *Hannibal.* New York: Dell Books.

Harris, Thomas. 1991. *The silence of the lambs.* New York: Dell Books.

Hickey, Eric W. 2006. *Serial murderers and their victims.* 4th ed. Contemporary Issues in Crime and Justice series. Belmont, Calif.: Thomson Wadsworth.

Hock, Roger, R. 1999. *Forty studies that changed psychology: Explorations into the history of psychological research.* 3rd ed. Upper Saddle River, N.J.: Prentice Hall.

Howard, Pierce, J. 2006. *The owner's manual for the brain: Everyday applications from mind-brain research.* 3rd ed. Austin, Tex.: Bard Press.

Huckabee, Mike, and George Grant. 1998. *Kids who kill: Confronting our culture of violence.* Nashville, Tenn.: Broadman & Holman.

Hyde, Janet Sibley, ed. 2005. *Biological substrates of human sexuality.* Washington, D.C.: American Psychological Association.

Jacobs, Don. 2011. *Analyzing criminal minds: Forensic investigative science for the 21st Century.* Santa Barbara, Calif.: Praeger.

Jacobs, Don. 2009. *Brainmarks: Headquarters for things that go bump in the night.* Dubuque, Iowa: Kendall Hunt.

Jacobs, Don. 2008a. *Mind candy II: Who's minding the intoxicated brain?* Plymouth, Mich.: Hayden-McNeil.

Jacobs, Don. 2008b. *The psychology of deception: Sexual predators and forensic psychology.* Plymouth, Mich.: Hayden-McNeil.

Jacobs, Don. 2007a. *Mind candy I: Who's minding the adolescent brain?* Plymouth, Mich.: Hayden-McNeil.

Jacobs, Don. 2007b. *Who's minding the adolescent brain?* Plymouth, Mich.: Hayden-McNeil.

Johnson, Steven. 2004. *Mind wide open: Your brain and the neuroscience of everyday life.* New York: Scribner.

Kalechstein, Ari, and Wilfred G. van Gorp, eds. 2007. *Neuropsychology and substance abuse: State-of-the art and future directions.* New York: Taylor and Francis.

Kantor, Martin. 2006. *The psychopathy of everyday life: How antisocial personality disorder affects all of us.* Westport, Conn.: Praeger.

Kiehl, Kent A., and Joshua W. Buckholtz. 2010. "Inside the mind of a psychopath." *Scientific American* 21, no. 4 (September/October): 22–29.

Komisaruk, Barry R., Carlos Beyer-Flores, and Beverly Whipple. 2006. *The science of orgasm.* Baltimore, Md.: Johns Hopkins University Press.

Larrabee, Glenn, J. 2005. *Forensic neuropsychology.* New York: Oxford University Press.

Larson, Erik. 2003. *The devil in the white city: Murder, magic, and madness at the fair that changed America.* New York: Vintage Books.

Lynch, Zack, and Bryan Laursen. 2009. *The neuro revolution: How brain science is changing our world.* New York: St. Martin's Press.

McGilligan, Patrick. 2003. *Alfred Hitchcock: A life in darkness and light.* New York: Regan Books.

Media Education Foundation. 2006. *Big bucks, big pharma: Marketing disease and pushing drugs.* Video, 46 min. Media Education Foundation, Northampton, Mass.

Meloy, J. Reid. 2002. "The 'polymorphously perverse' psychopath: Understanding a strong empirical relationship." *Menninger Foundation Journal* 66 (3): 273–89.

Miller, Bruce L., and Jeffrey L. Cummings, eds. 1999. *The human frontal lobes: Functions and disorders.* New York: Guilford Press.

Millon, Theodore, Erik Simonsen, Morten Birket-Smith, and Roger D. Davis, eds. 1998. *Psychopathy: Antisocial, criminal, and violent behavior.* New York: Guilford Press.

Otto, Shawn Lawrence. 2011. *Fool me twice: Fighting the assault on science in America.* Emmaus, Penn.: Rodale Books.

Patrick, Christopher J., ed. 2006. *Handbook of psychopathy.* New York: Guilford Press.

Patriot-News. 2011. "Jerry Sandusky's autobiography 'Touched' contains passages that now make the reader cringe." *Patriot-News,* November 12.

Pelusi, Nando. 2009. "The appeal of the bad boy." *Psychology Today,* February, 58–59.

Portales, Ashleigh. 2009. "Behind the monster's eyes: The role of the orbitofrontal cortex in sexually psychopathic serial crime." In *Analyzing criminal minds: Forensic investigative science for the 21st century,* by Don Jacobs. Westport, Conn.: Praeger.

Pron, Nick. 1995. *Lethal marriage: The unspeakable crimes of Paul Bernardo and Karla Homolka.* New York: Ballantine Books.

Raine, Adrian, and José Sanmartin. 2001. *Violence and psychopathy.* New York: Kluwer Academic.

Ramachandran, V. S., and Sandra Blakeslee. 1998. *Phantoms in the brain: Probing the mysteries of the human mind.* New York: HarperCollins.

Ratey, John J. 2001. *A user's guide to the brain.* New York: Vintage Books.

Read, Cynthia A. 2007. *Cerebrum 2007: Emerging ideas in brain science.* New York: Dana Press.

Ressler, Robert. 1992. *Whoever fights monsters: My twenty years tracking serial killers for the FBI.* New York: St. Martin's Press.

Restak, Richard. 2003. *The new brain: How the modern age is rewiring your mind.* Emmaus, Penn.: Rodale.

Ridley, Matt. 2003. *Nature via nurture: Genes, experience, and what makes us human.* New York: HarperCollins.

Ronson, Jon. 2011. *The psychopath test: A journey through the madness industry.* New York: Riverhead Books.

Rose, Steven. 2005. *The 21st-century brain: Explaining, mending and manipulating the mind.* London: Jonathan Cape.

Samenow, S. 1984. *Inside the criminal mind.* New York: Crown Publishers.

Schmid, David. 2005. *Natural born celebrities: Serial killers in American culture.* Chicago: University of Chicago Press.

Scholz, J., M. C. Klein, T. E. J. Behrens, and H. Johansen-Berg. 2009. "Training induces changes in white-matter architecture." *Nature Neuroscience* 12, no. 11 (November): 1370–1371.

Schoof, Renee. 2011. *Fort Worth Star-Telegram,* December 27.

The Science of Lust. 2011. Prod. James Younger. Documentary. Discovery Channel.

Simon. R. I. 1996. "Psychopaths, the predators among us." In *Bad men do what good men dream: A forensic psychiatrist illuminates the darker side of human behavior,* edited by R. I. Simon, pp. 21–46. Washington, D.C.: American Psychiatric Publishing.

Spoto, Donald. 1983. *The dark side of genius: The life of Alfred Hitchcock.* New York: Ballantine Books.

Stirling, John. 2002. *Introducing neuropsychology: Psychology focus.* New York: Taylor & Francis.

Stout, Martha. 2005. *The sociopath next door.* New York: Broadway Books.

Sullenberger, Chesley B. 2009. *Highest duty: My search for what really matters.* New York: Harper Collins.

Sykes, Bryan. 2004. *Adam's curse: The science that reveals our genetic destiny.* New York: W. W. Norton.

Toffler, Alvin. 1970. *Future shock.* New York: Random House.

Vaknin, Sam. 2005. *Malignant self-love: Narcissism revisited.* Prague: Narcissus Publications.

Walsh, David. 2004. *Why do they act that way? A survival guide to the adolescent brain for you and your teen.* New York: Free Press.

Wexler, Bruce E. 2008. *Brain and culture: Neurobiology, ideology, and social culture.* Cambridge, Mass.: MIT Press.

Whalen, Paul J., and Elizabeth A. Phelps, eds. 2009. *The human amygdala.* New York: Guilford Press.

White, Theodore H. 1975. *Breach of faith: The fall of Richard Nixon.* New York: Atheneum Publishers.

Zeidler, Eberhard. 1995. *Applied functional analysis: Main principles and their applications.* New York: Springer-Verlag.

Index

About the Authors

Don Jacobs is a professor of psychology and forensic science and chair of the Department of Behavioral Science at Weatherford College in Weatherford, Texas. His alma mater is Southern Methodist University in Dallas, Texas. He has published 30 works in psychology and forensic psychology, most recently *Analyzing Criminal Minds: Forensic Investigative Science for the 21st Century* (Praeger, 2011) and *Psychology of Deception: Analysis of Sexually Psychopathic Serial Crime* (Kendall Hunt, 2009). Professor Jacobs is coauthor with Nick Jacobs of a novel, *Freak Accident* (Kendall Hunt, 2002).

Ashleigh Portales is a crime-scene investigator for Denton County, Texas, and serves as adjunct professor in forensic and behavioral sciences at Weatherford College. She is a certified police officer in the state of Texas. Portales holds an associate's degree in forensic science, a bachelor's degree in interdisciplinary studies in forensic science, and a master's degree in forensic psychology.